How Parents Can Save America's Failing Schools

4217-PIER

How Parents Can Save America's Failing Schools

Gael Edward Pierce

14217-PIER

To order additional copies of this book, contact:
Xlibris Corporation
1-888-7-XLIBRIS
www.Xlibris.com
Orders@Xlibris.com

Contents

Acknowledgments 9

Preface 11

Introduction 13

Why Parent Help Is Necessary 14

Some Major School Problems 15

**PART ONE: WHERE OUR SCHOOLS ARE FAILING
THE HIDDEN CURRICULUM**

Learning Mythology 25

Testing 42

Some Questions to Ask 46

**PART TWO: THE SIGNS OF SCHOOL FAILURE
(INTERNAL CAUSES)**

Too Many Dropouts 49

Low Test Scores 52

Cheating 58

SAT Scores 60

Poor Employment Skills 62

Teaching, the Profession 63

Students Who Learn Differently 71

Illiteracy 83

Deteriorating Democracy 85

School Segregation 90

Some Questions to Ask 95

**PART THREE: WHY SCHOOLS ARE FAILING
(EXTERNAL CAUSES)**

The Pregnant Teenager and Single Parent 99

Unequal School Funding 103

Violence 109

Poverty — A major contributor to school failure. 113

Drug Babies 116

The White Flight 120

Home Schooling 121

In Summary 121

Some Questions to Ask 123

PART FOUR: SOME GOOD SCHOOLS

Teaching Reform 128

Curriculum Changes 136

Some Innovations 145

Some Questions to Ask 149

PART FIVE: HOW PARENTS CAN RESCUE OUR SCHOOLS

Checking Out the School 152

Meeting the School Personnel 154

Organizing A Parent-School
Advisory Committee 163

Financing School Reform 167

PART SIX: MAKING CHANGES

Programs to Increase Infant Learning 173

Helping Pregnant Teens 180

Curbing Teen-pregnancy 183

Curbing Violence and Crime 187

Reducing Poverty 189

Reducing Drug Usage 190

Reducing the Dropout Rate 194

Promoting Participation in Democracy 195

Some Questions to Ask 198

Community Learning Centers (CLC) 199

Enjoyment in Learning 205

REFERENCES 207

Education Publications 209

SOME BOOKS OF INTEREST 213

GLOSSARY 216

Appendices

A. Choosing A School 221

B. Help for Pregnant Teens
and Family Service Publications. 223

C. Programs to Teach Parenting Skills
HIPPY, PAT, BEEP, Head Start, Zero to
Three 228

D. Parent-School Organizations 230

Index 232

Acknowledgments

A special thanks goes to my daughter, Elin, who took time from working on her Ph.D. in biology to edit the manuscript and offer suggestions. My other two daughters, Nina and Alyta, also helped with discussions about their problems and success in home and school learning. I would like to report that all the teaching techniques offered by their father were successful and rewarding. Unfortunately, I was in the process of learning as were my children. They also had the distinction of attending school in a wide variety of locations ranging from Spain for pre-schooling, to schools in other foreign countries since I was working for the Department of Defense Dependents' Schools (DODDS) overseas. While they learned significant amounts in various areas, I found conversations with my three daughters about their daily classes, and my efforts to help them learn (unfortunately, not always positive), provided insight, both pro and con, in various areas of learning and teaching that would not be available to the average teacher.

There were also numerous people at the various schools who were kind and generous with their time and very helpful, particularly the special education personnel. A large number of school children and parents contributed to my understanding of problematic difficulties and the preschool importance in children's education. (G.E.P.)

PREFACE

When one considers in its length and in its breadth the importance of this question of the education of a nation's young, the broken lives, the defeated hopes, the national failures, which result from the frivolous inertia with which it is treated, it is difficult to restrain within oneself a savage rage. In the conditions of modern life the rule is absolute, the race which does not value trained intelligence is doomed. Not all your heroism, not all your social charm, not all your wit, not all your victories on land or at sea, can move back the finger of fate. To-day we maintain ourselves. To-morrow science will have moved forward yet one more step, and there will be no appeal from the judgment which will then be pronounced on the uneducated.

Alfred North Whitehead, *THE AIMS OF EDUCATION*— Presidential address to the Mathematical Association of England, 1916.

Part One provides information on the Hidden Curriculum and Part Two examines Signs of School Failure that are rampant in our school systems. Why Schools are Failing is dealt with in Part Three followed by an examination of Good Schools in Part Four. Part Five deals with important information on how Parents Can Rescue Our Schools and Part Six describes programs to increase infant learning plus reducing the problems of teen-pregnancy, violence and crime, poverty, drug usage and other school problems. The advantages of a Community Learning Center

(CLC) as a choice in school reform are also presented as a positive change.

Children are entering our schools in increasing numbers who, because of a lack of an early learning of social and emotional skills, are making teaching much more difficult and adding to the student dropout rate. Methods are presented here for helping parents establish techniques for infant and preschool learning to help those with at-risk offspring utilize early child development skills. Pro-active programs to teach the single parent techniques for improving learning skills prior to school entry are well established and are being successfully utilized in some homes today. Parents can remedy this major school problem of children with little incentive to learn, as well as remediate an increasing number of students with social and emotional behavior problems who are creating chaos in some classes.

The primary purpose of this book is to help concerned parents become aware of the need to check out their neighborhood school for quality conditions as well as areas that need immediate improvement. Specific methods are examined. There is also a desperate need to help expectant mothers in low income neighborhoods, as well as other mothers, to avoid depression and promote a healthful birth and a child free of debilitating problems such as fetal alcohol syndrome (FAS) and drug use while pregnant plus other preventable disabilities. The birth would be followed by trained resource personnel helping the parent incorporate successful methods for developing the child's verbal, social and emotional skills for success in school and later. The number of children entering school at an extreme disadvantage could be reduced by well established techniques. These programs have been available for quite some time, and are explained in Part Six.

INTRODUCTION

The fact itself, of causing the existence of a human being, is
one of the most responsible actions in the range of human
life. To undertake this responsibility—to bestow a life which
may be either a curse or a blessing—unless the being on whom
it is to be bestowed will have at least the ordinary chances of a
desirable existence, is a crime against that being.

John Stuart Mill, *On Liberty*, 1859.

It seems inconceivable that our school system has degenerated to
such an extent over such a long period of time. While some states
have been scrambling to improve our schools, minimum standards
are being increased to the highest level along with increased testing
for passing a grade or for graduation. Basically, we have a system that is
compulsory, with the children placed in a room with 20 to 30 other
children confined to desks and exposed to a curriculum they are
force to memorize from nine until three in the afternoon, and from
September to June. This arbitrary, forced learning, totally disregards
the children's interests and concerns—the basic factors in learning.

The purpose of this book is to convince the reader that our schools
are failing, and that the rescue and successful repair of our school
system will come from concerned committees of parents and others
who care enough to organize Parent-School Advisory Committees

14217-PIER

(PSACs) to make the necessary reforms in their local schools. Past government reform proposals appeared outstanding, only to be all talk with little improvement in our schools. Remember Goals 2000 by Presidents G. Bush (the elder) and Clinton? Where is it now? Turned over to the states. Without this effort by concerned parents, our schools will continue with very inefficient "education" programs that seriously affect a large percentage of our students with very poor learning skills. Today our society is increasingly divided between unsuccessful students and those who do well; about 30 percent get by, and about 15 percent do well. The rest either flunk out, drop out or quit trying.

Why Parent Help Is Necessary

What can we do about these schools? Put simply and starkly, I believe that those of us responsible for public education must never defend or try to perpetuate a school to which we would not send our own children. If a district has recognized that a school is in trouble and has given it help over a period of time and the school has not responded, we must shut that school down and start anew.

Sandra Feldman, president, American Federation of
Teachers. Sept. 7, 1997.

School reform movements have received much publicity, but little positive change has resulted. In 1983 a commission reported after an 18 month effort at a cost of $1,000,000: "Our nation is at risk . . . If an unfriendly foreign power had attempted to impose on America the mediocre educational performance that exists today, we might have considered it as an act of war." Today the solution suggested by everyone from presidents to principals is to raise test scores, assert more discipline, and offer more rigorous courses. Without parental concern and action toward saving our children and their schools, the separation will increase even more between successful schools for the children from middle and upper income families, and very unsuccessful schools in terms of test scores, graduation, and employment in the low socio-economic status (SES) neighborhoods. Schools in the lower income areas are stunted from the beginning. Children from these schools seldom receive the rewards of excellence found in upper income schools in terms of the number of graduates, further education, and employment. The educational spread between the middle and upper income families and the lower income groups is steadily increasing. Even while the wealthy group is increasing, the low SES group, often including two working parents with low salaries, is also increasing.

"The evidence seems clear that to close the gap in the quality of education, the community will have to do more than equalize treatment. Equal educational opportunity requires the application of unequal resources: more rather than less to the students from poor homes. Yet as a nation we are doing the opposite, spending much more money to educate the children of the well off than the children of the poor" (1). Milton Schwebel wrote this in November of 1967. Why hasn't the "quality of education" increased since 1968? There are a variety of reasons, none acceptable.

Some Major School Problems

An Outmoded System:
What does it mean for a student to do well or to fail? Schools that flunk a large number of students on a regular basis keep right on with no significant intervention to bring about meaningful improvement to help children learn other than by repeating the grade. Edgar Z. Freidenberg pointed out in, "Requiem for the Urban Schools" that the school situation was almost hopeless in late 1967 because the cities had neither the budgets, the personnel, nor the facilities to cope with the accumulated problems caused by years of neglect (2). And it hasn't improved to any degree since then. In 1983 a panel presented "The Nation at Risk," an evaluation of our schools which

15

described how poorly they were functioning. However, our school systems continued to decline. Candidates for public office from president to dog catcher have expressed concern for public schooling and suggested reforms—but there have been no significant changes in the majority of our schools. It is obvious that our school system will continue to "flunk" children from lower socio-economic status (SES) communities.

Inept Teachers: We have a national teacher shortage approaching 2.2 million, the US Department of Education estimated. We have schools that emphasize failure as the student's fault, suspension, expulsion and coercion as common practices in learning which violates numerous studies on what helps anyone to learn. The salary and prestige for teaching is incredibly low, and new teachers drop out usually within the first three to five years. Our schools need competent teachers. What amazes those of us concerned with the problems in children's learning is that this is not new; it has been going on for decades.

Inequality: While there have been movements against the property tax for school funding because it discriminates unfairly between the rich and poor neighborhoods, only two states so far have changed the financing of their schools. The decline in quality public schooling has been significantly affected by the growing poverty in the United States. The US General Accounting Office (GAO) at the request of Senator Carol Moseley-Braun, a Democrat from Illinois, found that "15 million students attend schools that need to be extensively repaired or replaced, and 7 million of our children attend schools with life-safety code violations, according to the GAO. It will cost $112 billion to up-grade our school buildings to good and safe conditions. According to the Department of Education we need to build 6,000 new schools over the next 10 years just to keep up with rising enrollment" at an estimated cost of about $200 billion. These are primarily in the low income sections of town.

Limited English Proficiency (LEP): The population of students with

LEP and English as a second language (ESL), if any English at all, are increasing in our schools. The Census Bureau (1998) predicted that children of immigrants will account for 88% of the increase of the under-18 population in the next fifty years. These children encounter problems in English language acquisition that result in the depletion of learning strengths that seriously affects how they learn in school. The response has been problematic with bi-lingual education replaced by a variety of other techniques. Bi-lingual really meant Spanish and English, since we had very few, if any, teachers who could qualify for any other language such as Hmong, Farsi, Tagalog, Yiddish, Arabic, Hebrew and a host of other languages.

In California over one and a half million children, or one fourth of the total school population, were not proficient in English. California's future depends on these children becoming fluent in English. The record, however, is not good. California's statewide Stanford 9 student test found students from affluent English-speaking families scored well above the national average. Limited English students make up about one-third of the states public school enrollment and most will be "at risk" unless test scores rise dramatically. They also risk failing California's high school exit exam.

Behavior Problem Students: A general behavioral pattern for many students who encounter difficulty in performing successfully in school emerges in the third or fourth grade. This leads to increased problematic behaviors, a cover for feelings of inadequacy, lowering self esteem and frustration. While a few students of upper income families may acquire behavior problem designations, the majority of students so labeled come from the lower income neighborhoods. These identified children are then put in special education classes. Most often the result includes dumbed down lessons, fewer hours in school, social rejection, and often dropping out of school between the ninth and twelfth grades. For many of these children juvenile hall follows, and since that institution seldom is effective in curing kids, prison is often the next residence.

At Risk Children: Twenty years ago the children referred to me as a school psychologist by the teachers and other school personnel most often were from the 7th and 8th grades. Today, the children in the first and second grades are referred to specialists regularly, and the number is increasing. The Carnegie Corporation of New York after three years of research found that millions of infants and toddlers do not have the intellectual stimulation, medical care, and loving supervision essential for normal development. Adding to the difficulty will be an increasing number of students born to single, teenage parents who have severe behavior problems as class sizes increase and money for special education classes decreases. Every year nearly 65,000 teens have babies in California — that's one birth every eight minutes. At risk children are increasingly more difficult to teach and are raising school expenses.

Another source of At Risk children comes from chemicals in the environment that cause problems as the number of childhood learning problems soars. Various sources have discovered evidence that compounds such as polychlorinated biphenyls, (PBS) can result in a lack of coordination, diminished IQ, and poor memory among children. Children who are subject to this involve one of every six in America and suffer from various disabilities such as autism, aggression, dyslexia, and attention deficit hyperactivity disorder (ADHD). In California, reported cases of autism rose 210 percent from 3,864 to 11,995, between 1987 and 1998. In New York the number of children with learning disabilities jumped 55 percent, from 132,000 to 204,000 between 1983 and 1996.

Lack of Early Education: A primary reason for school failure is the increasing number of children primarily from low income areas who do not receive the essential care in pregnancy, and stimulation for learning in their early years, either due to a lack of parental skills, single-teen parent, or other parental reasons. Programs to help all children learn verbal, social and emotional skills prior to school entry are a vital necessity. Early learning from birth to age five is the most important learning in the child's life. Unfortunately, this early learning is ignored in most low income families.

The students I worked with in a residential institution were sent there for petty crimes, desertion by parents, drugs and other problems. Many had IQ scores ranging from brilliant to borderline retarded, but their personalities due to a lack of social and emotional skills were nearly all dysfunctional. This pattern must be changed as this school population continues to grow. The number of these children in public schools who end up in institutions is increasing at a rapid rate as the traditional, two-parent family continues to decline and the teenager, with single-parent offspring, becomes more prevalent. These children enter kindergarten with virtually no academic skills and little, if any, training in social and emotional abilities so necessary for successful adaptation to school and life. These students do not have a fair chance at school or social success without early help. Why hasn't this major problem been dealt with long ago?

Testing: Schools have changed into test passing centers. There is a national trend to focus the curriculum and teaching to specific standards to enable students to pass tests since schools and districts are being held accountable for the students' "achievement,"— a test score. While the middle and upper income level families will, no doubt, have children who will succeed since many are already involved with GPA and SAT scores to enable them to get into a college, the majority of the other students will find school even more uninteresting and demanding, and far from fulfilling their needs.

Children in social groups who will not do well are children from the low income families and other children who have no long-range plans that involve good grades and graduation. Our schools have turned into forced learning centers when they should be involved in "learning" as the result of what the student finds interesting and worth exploring; not information being forced down the student's throat, particularly if the primary motivation for learning is the threat of failure and repetition of a grade—coercion.

The new emphasis on test scores and increased use of exams for promotion will increase the number of students who fail, increase the drop out rate, and increase the separation between the economic groups in our society. Parents need to become seriously involved in preventing this fiasco in their schools, but it will be difficult since the concept has been accepted by school people from President Clinton to the local principal who will get bonus money if his school improves its test scores. President Clinton was promoting "accountability," to stop "automatic promotion of failing students." The states that did not follow this policy were in danger of losing part of their federal funds. Wouldn't it be wonderful if the President also provided a cure for the students' failure rather than retention?

If the demand for test scores is impossible to avoid, then the suggestion should be for test scores from the beginning of the school year compared with test scores at the end of the year. As it is now, the exams given at the end of the year only measure only what the test creators reasoned were important facts to memorize. What we really should be interested in and want to measure is how much farther along the learning line the pupil moved during the school year; what the student learned and didn't learn. This can only be measured by testing the student at the beginning of the school year to measure the learning the student gained the previous years, and then a similar test at the end of the current year to measure what information has been memorized for this learning year. But this again places an undue emphasis on a very small amount of learning indicated by test scores, not learning overall.

See Part One for more on testing.

Responsibility: One of the basic, long-term problems with our public schools is the difficulty in determining who is responsible for the failure of students to learn and the large dropout rate. The line starts with the teacher, the principal, the district superintendent, the city mayor, then to the state school board, the superintendent of public instruction, an education secretary or equivalent, and governor. The next step is to determine what their duties are individually. In most states these duties overlap or are ill-defined. In California over the past 25 years court decisions and voter initiatives on the ballot changed the control of the public schools from local districts to Sacramento.

The California Constitution gives Sacramento control over school financing, including the level of state and local revenues going to schools. Why should Sacramento dictate that districts buy textbooks, even if they don't need them, or risk losing the funds? The locus of control should begin with the school. Our California school system is overloaded with a large state education code with rules and regulations that have blocked school improvement rather than stimulate it. In the meantime, schools are being held accountable for poor student achievement when they have little control over what programs are required by the state and the personnel available to carry out the mandates. There is no clear policy on getting rid of inept teachers.

One suggestion was to trim the voluminous state education code, which is the bane of many school districts since the rules do more to restrict the flexibility that is so important to improving the schools. The question asked was, "How can districts be held strictly accountable for student achievement when they have little or no latitude over so many program decisions, not to mention the power to manage personnel?" California has a state school board, a state superintendent of public instruction, and an education secretary with ill-defined duties. Any rescue effort, however, will be very difficult without the cooperation of the teachers' unions, the education bureaucracy and the legislature, all of which are largely responsible for the sorry state of California's schools.

Groups should investigate the controlling organizations involved in their schools district, and evaluate their effect on the schools' efficiency. Many committees will be amazed at the number of groups who determine educational policy, and the lack of basic responsibility for the failure of the school system. Next examine where the school funding is distributed in your district and state. Our success or failure as a society in the 21st century will largely depend upon whether we continue to ignore these school problems or confront them.

PART ONE

WHERE OUR SCHOOLS ARE FAILING

The Hidden Curriculum

While the external problems place a tremendous burden on public schools, the blame can not be placed entirely on outside circumstances; much of the failure is problematic to the school system itself and inherent in the daily operation. How and why children learn most efficiently has been common knowledge for a long time, yet our schools turn off children's interest in learning, often due to the outmoded teaching techniques that have been described as The Hidden Curriculum; the inherent lessons we don't want our children to learn.

> I am using the term Hidden Curriculum to refer to the structure of schooling as opposed to what happens in school, in the same way that linguists distinguish between the structure of a language and the use which the speaker makes of it.
>
> Ivan Illich, *DESCHOOLING SOCIETY,* 1971

So it is in medical school: Attitudes and values are shaped far more by the so-called invisible or informal curriculum than by the formal curriculum.

Charles Silberman, *CRISIS IN THE CLASSROOM*, 1970

In this country, public education has traditionally been closely connected with the world of work, and the continuing effect of this relationship can easily be seen if one examines the school's covert curriculum . . . The Covert Curriculum has not changed since the public schools came into existence.

C. A. Bowers, *CHANGING EDUCATION*, 1972

The lessons of the Hidden Curriculum are part of every school program, and will be absorbed by the children unless precautions are made to make sure this doesn't happen—and then it's not easy. The lessons are transmitted via the very process of school, the inability to change, how the subjects are taught, and the institution of school itself. These lessons are learned by experience and exposure. Some lessons are part of the make-up of school in its technical operation and have been for many, many years, while other lessons in the Hidden Curriculum are the result of the misconceived beliefs transmitted unconsciously.

Learning Mythology

The Myth: School Promotes a Desire for Learning

No matter what subjects students are required to take, students will want to learn them.

"If we claim the primary goal of education is to develop every person's natural inclination of inquiry, we would have to admit that despite the enormous output of the American educational system, we have come nowhere near that goal, and perhaps, indeed, have been traveling in the opposite direction." C. West Churchman pointed out that only a few talented people really knew how to inquire objectively. He blamed the required courses that view education as information-processing "that will build up a student's memory bank." But if the main purpose of education is to develop each individual's "natural inclination to inquire, there should be no required courses at all, even though it is possible that everyone will need arithmetic as well as a natural language through which to communicate" (1)

A 1965 Nobel prize winner in physics said he doubted if schools would be better off *not* to educate children in such subjects as math and science; that if they were left alone, the students would, maybe by accident, find a good book or an old textbook or a TV program that would turn them on to that subject. "But when youngsters go to school, they learn that these subjects are dull, horrible, and impossible to understand. I knew before I got there that math and science were interesting. All I saw was that they were dull in school." Richard Feynman, a professor at California's Institute of Technology and a best selling author, added: "Someday people will look back at our age and they'll think, 'My goodness, how they tortured their children!' Yet look how easy it is to teach. But they didn't know it back then" (2).

The Myth: Testing Reveals Learning
We can tell what students have learned and how much by testing.

The ability to correctly answer questions that have little meaning or bearing on the student's life has long been equated with acquiring knowledge. But what testing measures, the selecting of the correct response to usually one of four or five choices, is an understanding of how-to-play-the-game. Some students have the motivation and resources to play the game with zeal, but many others see no reason to spend half an hour or more trying to figure out complicated questions that have no relationship to their lives or interest.

All tests are not the same in terms of the value of assessment, and to accurately measure what is being learned, a variety of statistics need to be known. For tests used on a wide scale, the user must understand some essential data before the test is considered valid. What group was the test normed on? To achieve "standard scores," the test had to be normed on some students. What ethnic groups were in that sample? What is the validity of the test? To be reliable, how would the group do if they took the same type of test a number of times? To be valid and reliable, tests must include the background of the individuals on which the test was normed, as opposed to a national test for everybody with the assumption that it fits every student as a measurement of ability, and the data must have been gathered over a long term.

The Myth: Obedience is the Most Important Learning Behavior
In order to learn in school, students must never question, just obey, and do what they are told.

We all want our children to obey, to follow the rules, and do what they are told, but as Postman and Weingartner wrote, "Couldn't we accept children without blind obedience? Is it necessary for our survival to continue producing unquestioning children and adults?" They pointed out that the voice of authority was to be trusted and valued more than independent judgment in schools, and that one's own ideas were inconsequential (3). Urie Bronfenbrenner described it as children growing up in a context of "obedient, submissive, and likely to conform to the morés of the group in which they are reared, but the problem is this; men and women in our society are supposed to be independent, aggressive, and self confident and strong" (4).

In many classrooms humiliation is used as the main method of control and enforcement of the work ethic. The child is held up to ridicule with no opportunity for self defense or rebuttal. Those that do answer back are sent to "the office." It is not uncommon to see teachers or administrators patrolling the halls in schools or on the playground, not to encourage children in their activities, but as wardens looking for offenders of the system. We have the command,

"Line Up!" and other confinement characteristics (bull horns, metal detectors, hall monitors) typical of public schools and prisons.

Students must follow some basic rules, but blind obedience is another issue. The disciplinary tactics in many schools are a result of the needs of teachers, and have little relation to the learning process. Dissent is acceptable, especially in a democracy where it is a requirement. It is necessary to follow the rules, but it is also important to examine and even question those rules. If this didn't happen, blacks in Alabama would still be riding in the backs of buses and women wouldn't be allowed to vote.

The Myth: Coercion Promotes Learning

The best way to keep class control and to promote learning is to utilize dire punishment.

Infants want to know. They want to learn, but they must be in control, and they must let us know by their interest when to continue and when to quit. They learn how to coordinate muscle growth, how to grasp, walk, and speak all on their own due to a basic need from within. In school, however, children are told they must learn at a certain time and place, a certain amount, and if they don't they will be subject to coercion such as poor grades, letters to their parents for behaviors judged adverse, plus detention, paddling, suspension, retention and/or expulsion. I've never figured out how these improve learning. Most teachers use coercion for class control and would argue that it is necessary to keep the bad kids in line and the good kids working.

Like the infants, older children have to understand that learning a subject is in their best interests and coincides with their goals. If it doesn't, the coercion won't transform the subject matter into interesting learning. Teachers can find the students' interest areas along with their level of understanding of the subject, and make learning personal and non-coercive. The motivation to learn must come from within. William Glasser has shown that by treating the disruptive children as members of the class and asking class members how the problem should be handled, among other techniques, coercion can be reduced. Many teachers, however, could not function without coercive control. Very often the child who is treated with coercion responds in kind, overtly or covertly.

The Myth: Corporal Punishment Corrects
Spanking bad kids will make them good.

The National Association of School Psychologists (NASP) indicated that more than half our states ban the use of corporal punishment, yet almost a half million children each year were being hit or spanked in public schools with a disproportionate number being minority children and children with disabilities. Any intervention which is designed to cause pain in order to stop or change behavior is corporal punishment. NASP reaffirmed its opposition to the use of corporal punishment in schools, and stated it will actively support removal of legal sanctions for its use, " . . . (A)nd will encourage research and the dissemination of information about corporal punishment effects and alternatives." The Association pointed out that corporal punishment "(C)ontributes to the cycle of child abuse and pro-violence attitudes of youth by teaching that it is an acceptable way of controlling the behavior of others."

"Effective discipline is primarily a matter of instruction rather than punishment. . . . NASP reaffirms its opposition to the use of corporal punishment in schools and will actively support removal of legal sanctions for its use." They resolved to educate the public about the effects of corporal punishment and alternatives to its use, and encouraged research and the dissemination of information about corporal punishment effects and alternatives (5).

In February 1990, the US Congress heard testimony for the prohibition of corporal punishment for those students served under Public Law 94-142, the bill providing education for the handicapped. "The committee was advised that children in special education were paddled at least 132,000 times during the 1985-86 school year and that most of these students were males, poor, and too frequently, Afro-American. The Office for Civil Rights in 1984 reported that nationwide 24.5% of students were black, but 37.3% of corporal punishment cases involved black children. The subcommittee heard from the US Department of Education and the National Association of State Directors of Special Education that they opposed the prohibition of corporal punishment, seeing the issue as one of local control or that it would single out special education students for special treatment.

Corporal punishment was the second most-frequently used form of school discipline in Oklahoma, Georgia, Alabama, Mississippi, and Florida where it was supported by a majority of the citizens. Children in the lower grades were more likely to receive corporal punishment than children in the upper grades. Some states restrict the spanking to "the board of education," given by an administrator or designee, or the teacher with an observer, I guess, to count the whacks. Some schools do not designate anyone and even the bus driver could be called in to whack away.

The American Psychological Association (APA) in 1974 joined several other organizations by passing resolutions against corporal punishment in schools as did the National Association of School Psychologists (NASP). By 1995, twenty-seven states, many suburban upper middle class schools and most of the largest cities had banned it. However, at that time a large block of Southern states still paddled away. In fact, the United States may be one of the most punitive of Western democracies. Corporal punishment is not allowed in schools in Continental Europe, Britain, Japan, Israel, former Communist nations, Ireland, parts of Australia, Cyprus, Canada, Puerto Rico, Jordan, Ecuador, Iceland, Mauritius, the Philippines and the high school level in New Zealand. "In the home, Sweden, Norway, Finland, Denmark, and Austria forbid parental spanking" (7).

Some of the professional organizations that have taken a position against corporal punishment range from the American Bar Association to the American Medical Association. Any school that still administers corporal punishment is an example of an anachronism in education. This is one of the worst attempts at changing behavior, a throwback to antediluvian periods when education depended on fear and force, which still exists in many schools.

The Myth: Retention Repairs Learning

This myth states that the children who are doing poorly in school will improve and do better if they are flunked, held back or retained in the same grade, and try to learn the same subject matter again the following year.

Non promotion, or retention, has become the rallying cry for the proponents of back to basics. They advocate stricter promotion policies to reverse the trend of declining national test scores and increasing dropout rates brought to the public's attention in "A Nation at Risk: The Imperative for Educational Reform" (National Commission on Education, 1983). This rallying cry went over so well that by 1985 thirty-one states had mandated stricter promotion policies, others were considering doing so, and in those states that had not yet considered adopting such policies, retention rates were increasing. In some states by the eighth grade approximately 50% of the students had been retained. President Clinton called on all public schools to end the social promotion of all poorly performing students. He cited the Chicago program that "holds back" (read "flunks") thousands of students who failed to meet academic reading standards—on a test, of course.

If the child doesn't learn, for whatever reason, how can it be the child's fault and not the responsibility of those trained and paid to teach them? My teacher friends would advance all types of reasoning involving students who won't learn, refuse to cooperate, and those who are emotionally disturbed. The answer, however, is that our schools have the resources and techniques to help all children's learning interests and talents, plus counselors, special ed. teachers, psychologists and others. While there are some students who will not cooperate in learning algebra or memorizing historical data, they do have interests that could be stimulated to increase learning in areas that are meaningful to them.

A common reason given by teachers and educators for flunking a primary grade child are: "he's small for his age." That means he won't be noticed as too big in later grades with younger, smaller children. "He's immature." This means not ripe, but it is never really explained except for "sucks his thumb," or "pees his pants." He's "not ready." When you ask what will get him ready, the answer always is another year in the same grade—running him through the same process again—from beginning to end. Why will repeating the same grade again make him bigger, mature, and ready? What will be different this time through? Will he have the same teacher again? The same curriculum? What changes will be made to alleviate his learning problem? Very often when the child no longer sucks his thumb or pees his pants the second time around in the grade, those in favor of retention say, "See, he stopped the immature behavior." This reasoning correlates with Chauntecleer's claim that when he crowed, the sun came up. As a year older, the child would have most likely outgrown the immature habit regardless of flunking.

Protecting the teacher's ego is another reason for failing the child. When a child is promoted to the next grade and is unable to pass the mastery test of the previous grade, (can't spell, add, or read), the teacher who passed the child along must prepare for colleagues' comments such as: "Whatever did she do with Johnny all year? He can't even read at a K level or color between the lines!" When it comes time to face this criticism in the faculty lounge or flunk Johnny, Johnny is flunked and the teacher's ego and reputation are protected. Many parents go along with this get-even-with-the-child philosophy since they also have been convinced it helps. The parents team up with the teacher since they are unsuccessful in forcing their child to do school work at home for a variety of reasons. They agree with retention which only exacerbates the situation, and certainly doesn't provide the motivation for the child to do the work he or she is capable of doing. The result is lower self esteem with the child's thoughts about getting even or giving up. After spending many hours with parents of failing children, I found the cause for failure ranges from inept teachers to the student getting even with the parents.

The National Association for School Psychologists has a number of publications showing retention is harmful to children. Retention ranks with corporal punishment as one of the ancient anachronisms in education, both strong deterrents to meaningful learning and positive reinforcement. When we know learning is promoted by the child's interest in what is to be learned, why do we flunk children and call it beneficial? Research shows that repeaters rarely catch up with classmates and are more likely to drop out of school.

The Myth: Expulsion Expunges Sin
Kicking a kid out of school makes him think how bad he is, and he will never be bad again.

Suspension and expulsion have become common school punishments. Often "expelled," students are taught at home by a visiting teacher or transferred to another district or state. I have worked with school children in their homes because they have been kicked out of school for months at a time; one student had been out for three months. He had forgotten why he had been "expelled." The topper in a list of suspensions was that of a five-year old boy in kindergarten who "hit a boy with his knapsack." Wow! Five years old and suspended. But the boy *enjoyed* the suspension. It wasn't punishment to him, and the odds are he'll do something again to get suspended, if he can figure it out.

Zero Tolerance violation (guns, knives, drugs and other forbidden things) in school results in expulsion, and the child usually is sent to another school. Expulsion is a weird correction concept. As a learning institution, it seems reasonable that the school would examine the problem, the violation, and try to determine the reason and the remedy; not "get out of my house, forever!" This is a method of getting rid of the problem rather than solving it. What do children learn from expulsion? Don't get caught!

The Myth: Grades (A, B, C, D, F) Promote Learning

Children will strive hard to earn A's because competition and categorization by grade levels will encourage them to learn.

To most children grades are a threat; grades are not informative as to subject mastered or areas of deficit. The main function of the report card is to get the child in trouble with the parents when poor grades are brought home, and the parents find out for the first time that the child isn't producing in school. This myth of reporting a grade by a letter or a digit to tell how a child is doing in school will continue — it's part of our past — and future. Grades differ from teacher to teacher, school to school, and community to community. Some advanced schools have done away with grades by utilizing parent conferences and/or written reports about the student's progress.

If grades were the result of a basic norm or a series of norms by educators, then the grading process might be accepted by many critics. The teacher's grades result from random standards established by each teacher. These may range from readable handwriting to a developed vocabulary. Shouldn't every school or district have a uniform method of determining a student's grade, no matter what the subject? In many classes, the student's grade can be strongly influenced by good handwriting, neatness, spelling and seldom thinking or originality.

The Myth: The Textbook is the Best Source of Knowledge
Students learn subject matter best from a textbook.

Textbooks comprise about 90 percent of the curriculum. To sell a textbook, publishers must make sure that the book meets the largest possible market, which means the book can be read by nearly every child in the age range for which it is intended.

Much of the subject matter will be determined by the textbook the students are using, but they come from a virtual monopoly. In general there are five companies—Simon & Schuster, McGraw-Hill, Houghton Mifflin, Harcourt General, and Addison Wesley Longman— a majority of the market. While in theory the companies produce different texts to accommodate the needs of different states, the presidents of McGraw-Hill, Simon & Schuster, and Addison Wesley Longman pointed out that 80 percent of their texts content did not change much from state to state. Since California, Texas and Florida account for the largest percentage of book purchases, they get the most attention in needs. Critics claim that in order to keep each state happy, the text covers too many subjects superficially. Try reading one sometime.

The Myth: School is an Equal Learning Process
School is a democratic institution where all children have equal rights in learning—it's up to them.

In his book, *THE GREENING OF AMERICA*, Charles Reich protested the categorization process when he described the government's direct efforts to influence consciousness via compulsory schooling. He believed that the American state was organized as a meritocracy, and produced two factors: a working force for the machinery of the state, and for those below, a condition of "inferiority" in which the individual assumes a lower role in the eyes of society and himself since he's not as good as someone who is successful. "It is the

35

meritocracy that makes the worker, white or black, (one) who despises himself." Our society has grown into a fairly stable hereditary meritocracy with social stratification formed by the distribution of "rewards." Those close in ability levels, for example college students, tend to marry and reproduce, and teach their children how to play the game. These are the ones who reap the social rewards (8).

Schools help to develop a few people who think of themselves as elite, as well as many others who think of themselves as less. The various school systems have implemented programs to identify the elite. These are called Gifted and Talented; in California it is known at GATE (very appropriate since it prevents others from getting in). These are the test takers in the upper two percent of scores or the 98th percentile. As you can guess, many parents spend a great deal of time trying to get their children into this prestigious group—which is about its only value since the "talent" side of the eligibility process is most often ignored. Beethoven couldn't make it into Gifted and Talented today if his test scores weren't in that top two percent.

The kids in this group belong to the National Honor Society, go to magnet schools, take National Merit Tests looking for scholarships, and know how to play-the-game. Sometimes the gifted program has a "vaccination theory" approach; take the kids out of class on certain days and give them a shot of giftedness training.

Nearly all of us feel that those "above us" in positions of power or income know more than we do; that they possess the ability to understand complex concepts we find difficult. This irrational belief is fostered by the meritocracy belief in our schools.

The Myth of Competitive Learning

Children learn best by competing with one another for grades and recognition.

This myth is apparently the outgrowth of the Westward Movement, rugged individualism, and capitalistic competition. The myth promotes the idea that school is some kind of a race, and that the fleet of foot will gain the A's and the less fleet the F's. Too bad, but that's the way our competitive society operates. But every contestant doesn't begin at the same starting line. Some have a slight advantage and others a monumental head start. (No pun intended on the early education program.)

All children want to learn, but placing them in a contest to see who can memorize the "necessary facts" of a dull subject is wrong. When self esteem is damaged, children look for other options. Grading students is part of this process. Most often the curriculum is handed down from the state level or district, but seldom, if ever, created as the result of local student interests or needs.

The Myth of Original Stupidity

This is the school myth that believes all children are born stupid and have to be taught; otherwise they will not learn.

What is ignored in this myth is that children learn much more outside of school than they do in it. Carl Rogers, an outstanding psychotherapist, wrote, "I have come to feel that the only learning which significantly influences behavior is self discovered, self-appropriated learning. We would do away with examinations. They measure only the inconsequential type of learning. We would do away with grades and credits for the same reason" (9). Schools believe all children must learn a basic core of knowledge because none of them could or would learn it on their own. Without this knowledge, children are considered dumb. (As neophyte psychologists in his class, we called Professor Rogers, "Dr. God.")

The Myth: School-Equals-Learning

If it isn't learned in school, this myth states, it isn't worth learning.

Dr. Allen, a former commissioner of Education who wrote about learning myths, called this the Myth of Isolated Learning. If there is

37

no certificate, diploma, or badge, learning hasn't taken place. This is one of the arguments against home schooling. I always find the importance of this myth interesting in the status given to a college graduate who can't find a job over a skilled machinist who earns a good wage. My father, who never graduated from high school, was a Class A tool and die maker with an amazing skill on machinery and in design. Bill Gates, the multi-billionaire, never graduated from college. Thousands of high school graduates are unable to find employment due to poor graduation standards and the school's reputation.

The Myth of Single Stratum Learning
Categorizing kids in groups based on ability will make them all smarter.

Tracking and homogeneous grouping is the practice of placing children in specific groups based on presumed ability levels derived from opinions of teachers and test scores. Reading groups are often formed based on the child's reading ability. Reading, however, is a complex process divided into a variety of skills: understanding what is read, pronunciation, phonics, phonics syntax, semantic phonemes, oration, word definitions, the ability to repeat the reading in the student's own words plus other areas. Our testing treats reading as a very limited subject. The basis for a good reading score and a poor one can depend upon what area is selected for determining the level of ability. A child may be good at phonics, for example, but not understand the story at all. In one reading test used in many schools, the reading consists of pronouncing some words, but there is no measure whatever of the meaning of those words. What we have then, is a test of pronunciation, not reading, but the scores are reported as reading ability.

The range of abilities of children in regular classes is enormous if we measured talents in phonics, spelling, repeating in the child's own words what has been read, writing original essays, and basics such as the ABC's, counting, and understanding numerical contexts. Children differ widely in ability levels. Our schools, however, give tests, and on the basis of the results assign children to special education classes where the children receive dumbed down assignments and lessons, a lowering of self concept, and a dislike for education because they are being told they can't handle learning as well as their peers. Children have talents and skills that are not measured by selective, limited testing. One autistic boy I tested showed me models of famous buildings in San Francisco and San Diego that he had constructed out of Lego—to scale. His verbal IQ was borderline retarded, but his performance IQ (ability to see it and put it together) was above average. It is not uncommon to find a child's abilities may be proliferant in areas not measured by formal testing.

Myth: Our Government Will Solve Our Educational Problems:

Our government will be successful in transforming our schools into efficient educational institutions. Much talk with little improvement merits a double F. One F is for posting unrealistic goals and the other F for the results.

One of the most notorious efforts at school reform in the US began August 26, 1981, when T. H. Bell, Secretary of Education, created the National Commission on Excellence in Education chaired by David Pierpont Gardner. In 1983 this commission provided a report titled, "A Nation at Risk: The Imperative for Educational Reform":

"Our nation is at risk. Our once unchallenged preeminence in commerce, industry, science and technological innovation is being overtaken by competitors throughout the world. This report is concerned with only one of the many causes and dimensions of the problem, but it is the one that under girds American prosperity, security, and civility. . . . What was unimaginable a generation ago has begun to occur—others are matching and surpassing our educational attainments. . . .

"If an unfriendly foreign power had attempted to impose on America the mediocre educational performance that exists today, we might have considered it as an act of war. . . . Our society and its educational institutions seem to have lost sight of the basic purpose of schooling, and of the high expectations and disciplined effort needed to attain them. This report, the result of 18 months of effort, seeks to generate reform of our educational system in fundamental ways and to renew the Nation's commitment to schools and colleges of high quality throughout the length and breadth of our land."

Indicators of the educational risk the 1983 commission found were similar to those being pointed out today:

- *International comparison of student achievement completed a decade ago (1973) found American students were never first or second in 19 academic tests compared with other industrialized nations but were last seven times.*
- *Over 23 million adult Americans are functionally illiterate by the simplest tests of everyday reading, writing and comprehension.*
- *About 13 percent of all 17-year-olds in the United States can be considered functionally illiterate, and this illiteracy among minority groups may be as high as 40 percent.*
- *The average achievement of high school students on most standardized tests is now lower than 26 years ago when Sputnik was launched.*
- *Over half the population of gifted students do not match their tested ability with comparable achievement in school.*
- *The College Board's Scholastic Aptitude Tests (SAT) demonstrate a virtually unbroken decline from 1963 to 1980. Average verbal scores fell over 50 points, and average math scores dropped 40 points. Both the number and proportion of students demonstrating superior achievement on the SAT's with scores of 650 or higher, have also declined dramatically.*
- *Between 1975 and 1980, remedial mathematics courses in public 4-year colleges increased by 72 percent and now constitute one-quarter of all mathematics courses taught in those institutions.*

- *Business and military leaders complain that they are required to spend millions of dollars on costly remedial education and training programs in such basic skills as reading, writing, spelling, and computation. The department of the Navy, for example, reported to the Commission that one-quarter of its recent recruits cannot read at the ninth grade level, the minimum needed simply to understand written safety instructions. Without remedial work they cannot even begin, much less complete, the sophisticated training essential in much of the modern military.*

The co-chairman of the panel who wrote this 1983 landmark report, Glenn T. Seaborg, a former chancellor of UC Berkely and a Nobel prize winner, warned about the condition of today's schools and the sad state they are in. He pointed out that our schools have gotten worse since the 1983 report, and he blamed part of the problem on the poor quality of science teaching. "Educational content is continually diluted in a failed effort to produce palatable bits of information for progressively less skilled students." We appear to have declined rather than improved.

The Carnegie Commission after a thirty-month study (the National Commission took eighteen months) and at a cost of $1,000,000, reported that the National Commission on Excellence in Education had its "cycles confused." Their report guessed that about 15 percent of American high school students were getting the finest education in the world, but about twice that number were merely marking time in school or dropping out. The majority of students, the report indicated, were somewhere in between, attending schools that may have some good classes, but where generally there is little intellectual challenge. Both reports indicated teachers had a bad deal in pay, status, and working conditions. But, of course, this was being ignored in the rush to extend the school day and year as the National Commission recommended.

*   *   *   *

41

Why do the schools maintain this mythology even though many educators are well aware of the falseness of the premises? If changes are to improve our educational system, parents need to become involved in the rescue, or the issue will remain a political debate with much discussion and few positive results. A casual observation of our school improvement over the past few decades will reveal a continuous degeneration of learning and interest in our public schools. Our governments, state and federal, have repeatedly demonstrated a preference for upper income neighborhoods and the quality of their schools, and rejection of the students and schools that need help the most—those in the low income regions. The conclusion is obvious. . . . Parents are the last positive resource for saving our schools.

TESTING

I never let schooling interfere with my education.

Mark Twain

National Testing: This program would require all schools to administer the same test(s) at the same times to the same grade-level students and compare results. The argument for National Testing Standards states that it would produce "accountability" for educational performance in every state, and a program for educational reform. National Testing would have to meet "world-class standards" and be part of a "national curriculum."

Mainstream reformers ranging from Chester Finn of the conservative Hudson Institute and Diane Ravitch of the centrist Brookings Institution to liberals like the late Albert Shanker of the American Federation of Teachers have embraced standards and testing; so have Presidents Bush (both) and Clinton. The main argument suggests that testing and standards provide a basis for parents to know how well their children are doing, and how they compare with others in the same grade. Still, if a child is performing at the class level, but the class isn't near the national level, then there is a problem.

National testing assumes every test taker has received learning in certain areas that involve the basis of the test questions. It also assumes all students are equivalent in their understanding of the language of the question, in test-taking experience and in desire to perform up to par. It also assumes that the curriculum is equal in all schools, and that teachers will not teach to the test and the principal will not raise the student body scores.

President Clinton, a good test taker, promoted national testing as a way to evaluate schools—better test scores equal better learning when there is still serious argument about what constitutes learning. Clinton's emphasis was on improving reading and writing, both of which have not increased in test score results over the years according to the Education Department's National Center for Education Statistics. The Republicans are afraid this national testing would be the first step in a national curriculum. President Clinton's reply was, "We all know we have more to do to improve our schools and to raise learning levels for all our students. I've been working to improve education for nearly 20 years now, and I am convinced we can give our children the education they need to thrive in the 21st century only by challenging students, teachers, parents and principals to meet them."

But guess who will do the improvement in test scores—those students from the middle and upper SES groups who will work to improve their scores. The others from the low income areas—those who do not do well now—will continue to get poor scores unless some changes are made early in their lives. They also know from past experience that "testing" is not for them.

Teachers and Testing: Teachers are trapped into the testing game, and most would not know how to evaluate a student without a test. They believe the tests actually measure what the student learned. But we all know that teachers never test in April what they taught in October. Why? Because without a review the students would fail because they can't remember what they "learned" in October six months later unless there was some "assimilation and correlation" of the information in their understanding as Jean Piaget would say.

So we go along faking the testing game and becoming entrapped in the fakery. If teachers were freed of the tyranny of testing, they would still hew close to the curricular lines, but at least they would be stripped of the excuse of kneeling to central office policy. The test and the text are the two most important, most used, measurement functions in education today. Very few teachers would operate in class without one or both.

We have students who are ruined by testing; who have their self concept demolished, their plans for the future put on hold, and make teaching them in class often in an impossible proposition. Many get even in a variety of anti-social ways from outbreaks in class, drugs, violence and rebellion. The most reasonable method to create learning in all students would be to make the learning meaningful for each and every student so that the student would be enticed to learn, not punished for failure to absorb facts and details that have little to no interest or concern for him at all. It is incredible to many of us that our schools have never learned how to interest children in learning, but instead grade them on standards devised by "experts" in another community or state.

California has an exam required to be passed by all students in order to graduate, the High School Exit Exam (HSEE). The state law requires that California public school students must pass the exam to receive a high school diploma, beginning with the class of 2004. But the previous year, 2000, only 34 percent of the ninth-graders passed both the math and English language sections. This is reducing education to passing a test, and that means the good test takers will get a diploma, and the vast majority of Limited English Proficiency (LEP) students and those who dislike test taking and/or slow learners, will all fail to graduate. Does it make sense for children to attend school for four years, learn a wide variety of information from reading to geometry, and then be rated on how they answer some selected questions that could have little bearing on what they learned overall. How can a student be rated after four years of learning on a two hour test? How can the state legislature require LEP students and others with limited learning skills to be compared with those who speak the language from birth and who do well on tests?

In addition, some teachers were giving the test and allowed lunch breaks. Obviously, the children will discuss the test and trade information. Some students took the test in the morning and accomplished more correct answers than did the students who took the test in the late afternoon. It is amazing that a student's entire school career could hang on one questionable test particularly when the teachers giving the test use entirely different test methods. Some keep the students in the room for two hours without a break; others test in a gym on the bleachers.

If parents want to keep their children from taking the tests, they can run into a great deal of difficulty. Some teachers have refused to administer the STAR test to LEP students who are not fluent in English. Some teachers let the parents of LEP students and others know about the testing and suggest keeping them home on test day. Some teachers encourage students to refuse to take the test—but all of these methods of test avoidance are violations of California law which gives detailed instructions on what is legal and illegal for parents and teachers who try to keep children from taking the test. It is unbelievable that a legislature so far from the classroom would enact laws on test taking for ALL children. California is not the only state where the students are all treated as if they all came from the same environments. It's a given fact that the students in the low income areas will do much more poorly than those students in the middle and upper income neighborhoods.

Students have individual differences beginning with successful prenatal growth and parent involved preschool learning. Many stu-

14217-PIER

dents, however, do not have this preschool advantage. They are the ones who will do poorly on the tests, many of whom will not graduate. For a legislature to place this onus on these children who are easily identified by the third grade, is a crime. There is little doubt that it will build the dropout rate. See *The California Educator* November 2000.

Some Questions to Ask

1. Does your school use corporal punishment? What types and how often?
2. What is the school retention rate — also class by class? What is the expulsion and suspension rate? Are there some teachers who set the record and others who don't contribute?
3. Do minority students have any success in school in grades, graduation and punishment? Are they elected to class offices?
4. What qualifies students to be placed in "tracks"? Do all have the same qualification? Are the tracks effective in improving learning, grades, and graduation?
5. Do school personnel take seminars or important courses? How often?
6. Is cultural bias evident in promotion, retention, gifted and other areas?
7. Is there evidence of positive reinforcement, awards, etc.?
8. Are any teachers members of the Board of Education? Most likely, no.
9. What's the school's failure rate by grade and ethnicity?
10. What different economic districts make up your school population? Does the student population effect the teacher school curriculum?—or the rules and regulations?

See Appendix A for more questions.

PART TWO

THE SIGNS OF SCHOOL
FAILURE

(Internal)

Though this be far from being a complete treatis on this subject, or such as that everyone may find what will just fit his child in it, yet it may give some small light to those whose concern for their dear little ones makes them so irregularly bold, that they dare venture to consult their own reason in the education of their children, rather than to wholly rely on old custom.

John Locke, *On Politics and Education*, born 1632.

One of the most outrageous things about failing schools is that everyone—including the district administrator—knows which ones they are, but often years go by and no one does anything about them. In some cases, a school's problems are obvious. There is chronic disruption and violence, poor attendance, filthy hallways, and of course, achievement that is consistently below par. But sometimes a failing school is just a dead place where everyone has given up.

Sandra Feldman, president of the American Federation of Teachers (AFT) 1997.

While there is general agreement on the failure of the American schools, Part Three deals with some specifics of school failure that should be checked out in every school.

Too Many Dropouts

If the goal of public education is to have each student remain in school, learn the basics and graduate, then the grade for our system is surely an F. Our dropouts prove it.

> One-third of those now in high school will not graduate. "Our educational system has been the most ambitious in history . . . (yet) today 28 percent of our young people are not graduating from high school, and in the last twenty years the number of dropouts has increased nearly 100,000 a year to a total of 700,000 a year. Most high school dropouts are from our major cities—seven of which have dropout rates in excess of 30 percent. New York's rate, for example, is 37 percent; Detroit's 38 percent; Philadelphia's 47 percent."

> *Saturday Review,* May 1969

There are multiple signs of teaching-learning inefficiency in our public schools, and the growing dropout rate is one of the top three. Many educators, however, would deny that dropouts signify a problem, but the logic seems to be that the purpose for sending children to school is so they may learn, and in order to do this they must attend class. If they choose not to attend, in nearly every case, it would appear to be the fault of the schools and teaching because the child was not inspired to learn and chose to leave. The dropout usually is the student who finds school very difficult by the fourth grade, suffers lowered self esteem, has tried alternative ego-boosting techniques which were often anti-social (gangs, pregnancy, drugs, fighting), and then quits.

About 2,000,000 students, an incredible number, drop out and join the ranks of graduates without sufficient educational skills for little more than low paying jobs or welfare. The percentage of drop-outs has steadily increased. The problem has persisted in our schools over a long period of time and will continue.

The dropout rate in most districts is often more than the figure provided for public consumption. The dropout rate is difficult to determine, especially in districts in low-income areas where changing schools is more common. Many times the school is not aware of who is assigned to the school and who isn't. To avoid the look of an unsuccessful school, many schools and districts avoid the counts that are less than obvious, and this involves a high percentage of schools.

For example, in California nearly half of the students are considered from low income families, and almost 75 percent change schools at least once during their academic careers. More than 40 percent of the students are Latino, and according to federal statistics, Latinos historically have had a dropout rate roughly three times higher than that of the general population. A PBS television program on Oct. 2, 1998, reported that Latinos made up about 30 percent of the nation's dropouts with about 150,000 Hispanic children leaving school in 1997. The Hispanic dropout rate is 3.5 times higher than for non-Hispanic, white students; a monumental crime in our compulsory learning society.

High school dropouts experience more unemployment during their work careers, and young women who drop out of high school are more likely to become pregnant at young ages and more likely to become single parents. As a result of these factors, high school drop-outs more often end up on welfare and make a disproportionate part of our prison population. Our large dropout rate points a strong, negative finger at the schools' failure.

Dropping out is an expensive waste of human potential with few attempts to remedy the situation other than by coercion. Pre-drop-outs are punished in two ways: The inducement to return to school disregards any positive programs, but does: 1. Impose a fine or jail sentence or take away welfare payments if the parents can't get their children to attend school. 2. Take away the children's driver's licenses if they drop out. In West Virginia the state Supreme Court split 3—2 in upholding the nation's first law aimed at denying licenses to 16- and 17-year olds who fail to finish school. A program has been instituted in California that gives tickets similar to traffic tickets to parents whose children are chronically absent. State law makes parents responsible for children attending school which may work to get some children back inside the school, but guess what they will learn and how much cooperation they give to the learning. Instead of ordering the teacher and school personnel (counselor and psychologists) to look for the reasons why the child dropped out, and what could be done to make school more palatable and interesting, we order children back into an environment that was unsuitable and unpleasant or suffer punitive actions. How can threatening actions and coercing children to attend school take place in a "learning institution"?

There is little doubt that formal education in this country has been terribly eclipsed by those forces that are now actually educating the majority in their formative years—television, the mass media, and industry. The schools wait until the damage has been done, and foolishly suppose that their later efforts will redress the losses. The people who insist school equals learning are those who believe that in matters of the intellect, the mind is an inert blob that remains inactive unless "stimulated" (actually coerced) by school. In actuality we know the reverse is true. The mind is never at rest, even in sleep. The child is curious, seeking, trying to understand the difficult world, exploring, wondering, asking questions, and never a passive, waiting-to-be-turned-on type of mentality. It is, in fact, the schools that turn off the child. A twenty-five year study done in California found high IQ children (above 110) in the five to seven age range had a serious decline in IQ when retested in the seven to nine age range. Why? One of the most obvious conclusions was that the repressive nature of school and the "work, not play" atmosphere brought about a drop effort and in intellectual activity.

Milton Schwebel in 1968 warned in his book, *Who Can Be Educated?*, that the responsibility for the performance of children in school rests with the parents. "Society must assume ultimate responsibility for the performance of children who fail in school or who drop out." He also added that it was reassuring and convenient to attribute academic shortcomings to some qualities inherent in the child, such as low IQ or depressed motivation. "IQ's and motivation are not born, they are made. We make them, we the society, by many things we do—" (1). This is a very important conclusion, since most schools and parents feel that schools create the motivation, and as a result create children with sufficient IQ's. But the answer is that it is a societal process that begins with the child's birth and continues depending upon the "motivation" created in the child.

Low Test Scores

If the goal of public education is to create learned students who are able to pass standardized tests, local, state and national, the system has earned an F. (An F is always "earned," even if the grade results from no work at all.)

Some Test Results:

1.) The National Assessment of Educational Progress (NAEP) test was given to students in 37 states, the District of Columbia, Guam, and the Virgin Islands. Among the US students, Asians and Pacific Islanders earned the highest scores followed by whites, American Indians, Hispanics and blacks. The NAEP found that 43 percent of fourth-graders nation-wide did not have basic reading skills. In California the figure was 55 percent. The results were blamed on the large population of poor and limited-English speaking students. The late Al Shanker, president of the American Federation of Teachers, said, "Other countries have diverse populations as well. Why shouldn't people who are diverse do as well?"

2.) Among fourth grade students, 72 percent were able to add and subtract, but in the eighth grade only 14 percent had mastered seventh-grade skills involving fractions, decimals, percentages and simple algebra. Even in states with the best scores, only one in four of the eighth graders demonstrated the skills they were expected to have mastered. By the 12th grade only five percent of the students could do algebra and geometry, and less than half, 46 percent, could do eighth grade math. As students progress through school, their ability to achieve at grade equivalent test scores declined.

3.) Test scores released by the NAEP revealed that more than half of our high school students were unaware of the basic facts of American history, and were unable to use reason to back up their opinions. Education Secretary Richard Riley said the history scores proved the need for voluntary national academic standards. This is the standard remedy to improve our failing schools and raise our educational levels—higher test scores. This indicates a better rote memory in some students and nothing about stimulating student interest in learning, improving reading, or making learning meaningful. A report by the American Federation of Teachers supports President Clinton's suggestion for national educational standards, and indicated instruction and US test scores were far below the students' scores in Japan, Germany and France.

4.) The low US student performance levels were partly due to the percentage of students who were not taking advanced math. In Germany 26 percent of the students passed college entrance exams that contained a large math component. Over 36 percent of the French students did also, along with more than 50 percent of Japanese students. The closest comparison the US had was the advanced placement test for math which was taken by only four percent of the students and passed by two percent. Since all three countries, Japan, Germany and France, have national standards, this was given as the main reason for the students' better performances, which excludes more valid reasons such as concerned

14217-PIER

parental care in student success, particularly with Japanese students, different teaching techniques, different text books, and the amount of time in school. The textbooks used in the nations with the top scores were based on national standards specifying which concepts should be mastered at a given grade level. US textbooks are constructed to please a wide range of regional school districts. As a result the books are less than current and often designed to meet the needs of the biggest buyers—large school districts.

Instead of measuring reasoning ability, nearly all testing in our school system is a measure of rote memory, the acquisition of facts based on recall. We then rate the value of the school as a learning institution on the scores made on these tests. To do well on a test takes more than brain power; it involves being in the right mood, possessing the ability to concentrate, having an interest in the subject matter, and understanding how the game is played. For many students, playing the game by trying to solve meaningless questions that have no relationship to their world or interest is just not that important.

As a school psychologist, I have tested hundreds of children in order to obtain what I feel is a valid score. I must make sure the child is genuinely interested in taking the test and not merely faking it. If the child doesn't want to play the game to answer all those questions and solve all those problems, the final score will be much less than valid. Many children are tested who were never really concerned about the results of the test; only getting it done. The results, however, were often considered valid.

Some Test Scores: A study in 1996 among 41 industrialized nations revealed the US students on the science section ranked 17th, and 28th in math. Data from the Third International Mathematics and Science Study gained significance due to the most ambitious international comparison ever done. Most of the industrialized world beat the US in math, and only Spain, Greece and Portugal had lower marks. Singapore was in first place, Japan ranked third in math scores, and this was attributed to the way the subject was taught with Japanese teachers using open ended solving of problems that were not cut and dried, and permitting various methods to arrive at problem solutions. "What we're teaching in the eighth grade, Germany and Japan teach in seventh," said Pascal Forgione, US Commissioner of Education statistics.

The Third International Mathematics and Science study taken by about 10,000 US seniors selected randomly from more than 200 public and private schools touted as the most comprehensive international study of academic achievement ever, showed the following:

- Of 21 nations tested in high school math skills, the US 12th graders ranked 19th beating only Cyprus and South Africa.
- In a similar 21-nation test of science, our US 12th graders came in 16th beating only Italy, Hungary and Lithuania, as well as Cyprus and South Africa.
- Out of 16 nations taking the test in high school math, including those who had taken pre-calculus or calculus, the US 12th graders ranked 15th beating only Austria.
- Advanced science students in the United States ranked last in a similar 16-nation physics test.
- Seniors from the Netherlands ranked first in the general mathematics area, followed by seniors from Sweden and Denmark, and in the general sciences Swedish seniors ranked first, followed by the Netherlands and Iceland. President Clinton compared the poor senior scores with the strong performance by US fourth graders in the earlier tests. "This indicates that the cause of the decline in comparative scores is due to instruction, not student abilities."

Some test types:
1. Achievement test

This test measures memory. Nearly all IQ tests fall into this category whether admitted or not. Some of these tests have beautiful names such as CAT, DAT, STEP, SAT, ACT, TAP, ITBS: (Cognitive Abilities Test, Differential Aptitude Test, Sequential Test of Educational Progress, Scholastic Aptitude Test, American College Testing, Test of Academic Progress, and Iowa Test of Basic Skills). Unfortunately, there are many, many more. These tests are divided essentially into verbal and non-verbal forms. A proliferation of reading tests fall into this category as well as the Gates, Metropolitan, Iowa Silent Reading, Nelson-Dennis and others.

II. Aptitude tests:

These tests measure potential skills or development. They are really achievement tests in disguise. The aim is to find out if a student is ready for something such as algebra or first grade.

III. Intelligence Tests:

Speed and accuracy in solving problems is the primary factor. They are often called "learning ability tests." Some of these dated tests were the Lorge-Thorndike Intelligence Tests (verbal and non-verbal) and widely used; California Test of Mental Maturity, Otis Quick Scoring, Wechsler Intelligence Scale for Children (WISC), Peabody Pictorial, Henman-Nelson, Stanford-Binet, and so many, many more. Some are power tests that demand the questions be answered within narrowly defined time limits, while others are aimed at allowing the student to answer each question and have liberal time limits to enable the average person to try all the questions.

For a listing and description of the tests your children might be taking, consult Oskar K. Boro's *Mental Measurement Yearbook,* one among many that evaluate test types. This will give you a description of many of the tests, plus an evaluation from the statistics of the test's reliability, validity, coefficient of correlation, and other pertinent data. You will be amazed at how the tests that are given such unquestioned authority by the educators come off with such short shrift. For example, Boro's points out one short form test: "Does not give a factor analysis—other tests with verbal and non-verbal are better; (This test) "does not measure extremes at all well"; (This test) does not correlate in any way." It doesn't take much research to realize that tests, like IQ scores, are extremely relative.

IV. IQ Testing:

The forerunner of nearly all present day intelligence tests was the Metrical Scale of Intelligence devised in 1905 by Binet and the physician Simon. A fact of great, but often unrealized implication, is that the Binet-Simon test was commissioned by the Minister of Public Instruction in Paris for the explicit purpose of identifying children who were likely to fail in school. This work was mainly for the detection of mentally defective children, but the so-called "intelligence" Binet was trying to measure was actually "ability to do school work."

The 1937 revision of the Stanford Binet was standardized on 3,184 cases. The sampling was skewed toward children of upper classes and professional groups, and it included too few rural children and no "Negroes." Since an explicit attempt was made to include only test items which did not give an advantage to either sex, comparative studies can show nothing about the relative intelligence of men and women. When small differences were found, all they proved was that, in attempting to eliminate sex differences from their items, the designers of the test were only moderately successful.

Whenever a formal test is given, i.e. a test given on a wide school range, those giving the testing must be aware of the validity, reliability and the normative sample. Unless these data are known, there is no way the test results can be applied to a particular school or community. Those utilizing the test scores must also be aware of these terms since all tests differ in each area. For example, the normative sample must correlate with those taking the tests in school.

Cheating

The archaic method of measuring learning via test scores has resulted in some cheating, not so much by students but by teachers and principals, to improve the teacher's or school's reputation. Some administrators do this by making the test available to teachers in advance of the test date, or by changing the scores after the students take the test. A school in New York had the highest reading scores for five straight years until an official investigation found the principal had consistently changed wrong answers to correct ones—even those of a learning disabled student who scored in the 90th percentile. Some students get "practice tests" that have essentially the same questions as the "real" tests. Principals also ask that some low performing students stay home on test days.

A Columbia University study of more than 5,000 students in 99 US colleges found that at least 50 percent admitted cheating. The estimate today is that even more students cheat in high school. Cheating is more prevalent in high grade achievers than in low grade achievers since the pressure is greater at the top. It is really no wonder that our present school system based on lecture, assignment, and testing that learning has been divorced from schools, with today the goal of good grades and getting through. The students soon learn the mode of school survival; pass the test, get the grade; if you don't read the text book, that makes you one up on the system. "Man, I got a B in Pierce's history class and didn't crack a book all year!"

For most in education, the formula is something like this: We give a test in order to give a grade; we need a grade in order to determine how much the student has learned. The equation comes out: test equals grade; grades equal learning; high grades equal smart (success); low grades equal dumb (failure). The cry comes from the high school, "If we didn't have grades, how would the students get into college—on what criteria? It's the colleges' fault that we must depend upon an artificial system. It isn't the high school's fault. We're

bound by grade point average (GPA), class rank, and other requirements of college entrance." Tests and grades lead to an early educational demise without much doubt. Thus our system promotes cheating to survive. As long as teachers can hide behind tests they will not
feel the urgent need for reform on teaching methods. As long as
students sense that the test and test scores are what really count in
school, their main goal will be beating the tests and faking the game.

A test could have validity if it were taken by the student to see how
well he is learning for his purposes, not the teacher's. Once educators gain faith in our children's remarkable capacity to learn, they will
drop their dependence on these crude instruments. Final exams
can easily be replaced by long-term projects or written assignments.
Quizzes can be given for student diagnosis of learning problems, but
not for the teacher's grade book.

Testing has only two purposes: one is a whip to spur the laggards
on via fear, the other is a yardstick to show the laggards are lacking—
and fail. Tests can only measure a fraction of the months of learning.
Who can guess what the test maker will deem as important, or what I
find as absolutely incredible: a test produced by a national agency
that often has no correlation except in name with what the teacher
taught as important in that subject.

The data indicates ninety percent of the students from the lower
income families are totally ignored in school testing. At the elementary school level, these students find that testing for some students is
no sweat, but for them is difficult to impossible. They then learn what
is meant by "smart" and "dumb." The good grade getters snap through
the tests, are praised by their teachers and get "ooohs" and "aaahs"
from the class. Those that don't make the passing mark get sneers.
This is the beginning of the contributions to the dropout rate that is
over 50 percent of the students in many low income schools. These
are the students who are ruined by testing; who have their self concept diminished, their plans for the future abandoned, and make
teaching them in class often a difficult proposition. By giving up with

a lower self classification, many students get even in a variety of anti-social ways from outbreaks in class, drugs, violence and rebellion.

The most reasonable method to stimulate learning in all students would be to make the learning meaningful for each and every student so that all would be encouraged to learn, not punished for failure to absorb facts and details in which they have no interest or concern. It is incredible that our schools have never discovered how to interest children in learning, but instead grade them on standards most students have no interest or regard for, created by some outside agency such as the state education commission, or a national group.

Since test scores are often used to determine whether or not the school is successful in "learning," school personnel often use misleading years: "Our students' test scores improved 10 percent over previous testing," and the "previous testing" is any year in which the students did worse than the present test results. John Jacob Cannell found the "Lake Wobegon Effect" when the majority of the 32 states using national tests one year reported above-average scores at every grade level, a mathematical impossibility in a single year. A study by the US Department of Education supported Cannell's findings with "—school districts are presenting inflated results and misleading the public"—the Woebegon Effect.

SAT Scores

The SAT taken by juniors and seniors has been divided into two major parts, Verbal and Math. Before it was changed in 1996 the scores ranged from 200 to 800 with a total of 1600 for a perfect score. The College Board changed the average verbal scores on the new SAT from a score of 428 to 500, and the average math score from 482 to 500. The students from middle income and above families do much better on the SAT scores, which may be partly due to the dozens of commercial books for sale on *How to Pass the SAT*, as well as videos and seminars on the same subject. The test, however, does not predict student levels of success in college, and it has been cited as being biased in race and gender. The test results are only one part of the college acceptance picture.

In defense of the SAT requirement for admission to a college, the difference in grades from the various schools is cited, pointing out that a B grade in one school would only be a C in another, so that the SAT gives the college admissions people a better reference, and one to combine with the student's school grades. The argument against the SAT points out that it doesn't tell who will perform well at the university level, and it is racially biased in that it keeps out minority students who apply for college. SAT Scores have steadily declined over the years, and a variety of reasons are given by educators as the cause. More students are attending school which dilutes the data from the earlier "college bound" only students. More colleges are demanding test scores for admission which increases the numbers taking the SAT's, and the tests are harder, and so on.

The SAT also is declining in value as shown by the number of colleges no longer requiring it, nearly 100 since 1994. These colleges are placing more emphasis on course work and class rank, and less on the SAT and ACT—perhaps because high SAT score requirements reduce enrollment. Then why use the SAT as an admission criterion? Because a number in a verbal or a math test is simple, easy to read and less complicated than a long, wordy recommendation. Many colleges and universities combine the GPA and SAT scores, and many, if the GPA is top quality, do not require the SAT.

The national SAT scores show the Afro-Americans with the lowest verbal and math scores followed closely by the Puerto Ricans and Hispanics including Mexican Americans. While the whites have the highest verbal scores, the Asian or Pacific Islanders scored significantly ahead of the whites in math.

14217-PIER

Gael Edward Pierce

Poor Employment Skills

If the goal of public education is to provide students with an education that would enable them to find meaningful employment or an interest in further learning, the grade is D+. Students from the middle and upper income families do find employment and/or further learning.

At the National Education Summit, CEOs were concerned with finding workers who possessed the talent needed to learn vocational skills. Nynex tested 60,000 applicants to fill 3,000 jobs. Ameritech hired one out of ten job-seekers it interviewed since the others were unable to pass the basic tests in reading, math, and writing. Twenty percent of US businesses provide remedial training to employees, according to an American Management Association survey; in 1989 only four percent offered remedial classes. Motorola's CEO reported the company spends $1,350 per worker teaching basic skills. The smaller businesses can't afford this, and refuse to hire job seekers with only a high school diploma. A recent survey found only 18 percent of employers would hire a high school graduate for an entry level job.

As a result, businesses that rely heavily on education are pushing for local laws that force schools to set rigorous standards on what teachers teach and what students must learn in core subjects. The reasoning is that the CEO's will strive for national standards in testing to determine which schools are doing well and which ones are not. Other companies are pushing to change curriculums to add more science and math. The bottom line for the corporations is profit. As a group, companies provide grants worth $2 billion to all levels of education. They do, however, make sure the money is spent in areas that match the company's goals, called "strategic philanthropy."

The push for high standards in schools such as stricter requirements for graduation, including more algebra and geometry, are a primary concern of business. Otherwise, these businesses will have to pay the employees' cost of education. It is also one of the reasons our elected representatives push for higher school standards. This is part of the basis for the statements: "Higher standards" and "better test scores" from school officials. Businesses need qualified employees who do not require expensive training programs, and since corporations have a distinct influence on financing elections and government legislation, it is apparent that "passing exams for graduation" will continue to be a qualification for student promotions—unless parents intervene.

Teaching, the Profession

Learning is not filling a vessel.
It is kindling a fire.

Plutarch

One had to cram all this stuff into one's mind, whether one liked it or not. This coercion had such a deterring effect that, after I had passed the final examinations, I found the consideration of any scientific problems distasteful to me for an entire year.

Albert Einstein 1879—1955

The Need: School enrollment in 1997 reached a record 52.2 million students. Over the next ten years, high school enrollment is expected to have a 13 percent increase. The severe teacher shortage now facing our schools will require hiring more non-credentialed teachers, especially in urban areas that are plagued by poverty, violence and dropouts making them less attractive job sites for teachers. The Education Department estimated that we will need 220,000 new teachers per year for the next 10 years—compared with only 15,000 per year in the recent past.

But as we desperately need more teachers, how are we going to attract them? The schools are creating tougher teaching standards that compound the teacher shortage. Many of the present day education majors are flunking the low-level teacher licensing exams required by many states. The general request for smaller class sizes also increases the demand for more teachers particularly in California where the state invested $3.7 billion to reduce class sizes from about 30 to 20 in kindergarten to grade three. These classes most likely were taught by inexperienced and inadequately trained teachers, particularly in schools composed primarily of poor, minority and limited-English speaking students.

Teacher Quality: The National Education Commission (NEC) report estimated that the chances of a student having a mathematics or science teacher who is licensed in that field were less than 50-50. In the nation's poorest schools where hiring is most lax and teacher turnover is constant, the results are disastrous, the commission indicated. Too many children are taught throughout their school careers by a parade of teachers without preparation in the fields they teach, inexperienced beginners with little training and no mentoring, and short-term substitutes trying to cope with constant staff disruptions. It is more surprising that some of these children manage to learn than so many fail to do so. Nearly a quarter of all math students in grades 7—12 were taught by teachers who didn't take a college major or minor in math. An even higher percentage of biology students—39 percent—had teachers without even a minor in the subject they were teaching. To add to the problem, over half of all elementary teachers had classes larger than 25 students.

Solutions: The National Education Commission (NEC) recommended the nation set a goal of providing fully trained and credentialed teachers in every public school classroom by the year 2006. They also recommended raising salaries by linking pay to teachers' knowledge and skills, intensifying efforts to remove incompetent teachers, giving "low-wealth" districts the funds necessary to hire well-prepared instructors and providing incentives to enter teaching areas that suffer chronic shortages such as math and science. This sounds somewhat like the panel that wrote "A Nation at Risk" in 1983, listing all the faults of our educational system, with no significant improvements. But the NEC also included two representatives from the teachers' unions who were also against "merit pay," and who fought against any effort to loosen job-protection rules and "peer review" recommended by the commission.

Teacher training must be overhauled with more teacher education classes emphasizing the techniques of teaching that encompass the knowledge of motivating the students. As the number of students with problematic behaviors increases within the overall student body, our teaching staff is less qualified with less experience. This creates a very volatile situation in the classroom

Why does our nation continue to ignore the surmounting problems that make teaching a difficult job, ignore the children with serious problems, both physical and mental, that deserve our help to enable them to lead satisfactory and meaningful lives? Why aren't there increasing protests from members of our communities pointing out this sinful practice of ignoring meaningful methods for improving the lives of unfortunate children? We give up, fail these children, and impose harmful labels on them that result in further loss of self esteem.

Many states do not require prospective high school teachers to pass tests in the subject they plan to teach. Isn't it interesting that while influential people in school performance are insisting that students be given more rigorous exams to pass from grade to grade, teachers are not. More than 29,000 California teachers are working with emergency credentials; some with no teacher training or experience. And guess what the state's solution is? Making higher standards that require more capable teachers than ever before. This is a basic problem facing our school children that is being dealt with in the typical bureaucratic fashion with contradictory solutions.

Beginning teachers should work with an experienced and successful teacher for at least one semester in an apprenticeship program, and then have colleague help during their first year of teaching. Most teachers will agree that it takes until the third year of teaching before they can relax in front of the class. Ongoing professional development for teachers is vital, and it should be more than taking the standard six units over six years as it was in one school district where I worked. The favorite three unit course for teachers was Administrative Problems, a course with no exams, for teachers aspiring to become assistant principals.

The chances of promotion for teachers are practically nil—once a teacher, always a teacher was our battle cry. There is job security, however, with tenure after one year or three years in some areas. After that, the teacher is home free since it is extremely difficult to fire a teacher for incompetence. In Milwaukee, out of a total of 6,000 teachers, not a single one was fired during a five-year period. Female teachers comprise 75 percent of the school population. Teaching and nursing, the two "feminine" professions which have the most to offer in terms of service to humanity, reap the least rewards in terms of status and salary.

Incompetent Teachers: The National Education Commission (NEC found that over 40 states allow districts to hire teachers who have not met any basic requirements. Less than 75 percent of teachers have studied child development, and teaching methods, and have degrees in the subjects they have been assigned to teach. Nearly one-fourth of all secondary teachers do not have a major or minor in their primary area of teaching. Only 500 of the nation's 1,200 education schools are accredited, and the commission found that education programs often fail to combine opportunities for practice teaching with theoretical studies.

The problems get worse as student enrollments reach their highest level ever and teacher retirements and attrition create substantial vacancies. More than 30% of beginning teachers leave in the first five years . . . More than two million new teachers will be needed by 2007.

Education Secretary Riley readily admits that schools have lowered their standards to fill teaching slots.

The California State Commission on Teacher Credentialing in May 1998 indicated one out of every ten teachers works without the proper credentials. In California there are 218,000 teachers and about 20,000 without teaching certificates. Credentialed teachers must have a bachelor's degree, a year of teaching methodology, pass a test on basic skills, and spend a semester as a student teacher — essentially the same qualifications I went through many years ago in California before I could teach.

The school location of the majority of the teachers without credentials reveals more of the problem. In well-to-do Marin County, CA, for example, only two percent of the teachers worked without credentials. In Los Angeles at the urban Compton School District, 49 percent were not certified while in Oakland 16 percent worked without a credential, and in San Francisco only eleven percent lacked the credential. While there may be good teachers who do not have a credential and inept teachers who do, the data indicate a major problem in our schools; the poor urban districts get poor, unqualified teachers. This, of course, is the locality that needs the most qualified teachers since that school population, in general, is loaded with school children most often lacking in verbal, social and emotional skills so necessary for school success.

Pay: During a recent period, the pay for all workers with bachelors degrees or higher averaged at approximately $45,000 per year, but for secondary teachers the average was about $39,000. For beginning teachers the average was about $25,000 according to the National Center for Education Statistics. Obviously it is difficult to attract qualified personnel for teaching positions with sub-salaries; therefore, slots are filled with "emergency credentials." DeLaine Eastin who was California's Superintendent of Public Instruction, reported that California had 21,000 teachers on emergency credentials. This would not be tolerated in most business organizations that spend a great deal of time and money educating their personnel in the necessary procedures to make a business profitable and guarantee employee competence. Why is this permitted in a country so vocal about educating its children?

Janet Reno, Attorney General, in a speech to the League of Women Voters convention, said "Something is terribly wrong with a nation that pays its football players in the six digit figures and pays a lawyer going to Wall Street right out of law school $60,000 to $70,000 a year, and pays it school teachers what we pay them, considering what we ask them to do." She also pointed out that many of America's economic and social problems could be attributed to the under investment in how our infants and toddlers are brought up and trained. Teacher strikes are becoming more frequent as educational funding becomes less available.

Because the qualified teacher has become much more difficult to find, schools will continue to be filled by semi-to non-qualified teachers, and the ones we want will not be available due to the increasing school population and the lack of interest in teaching. This is another reason parents must become involved in their children's school, and why a Parent-School Advisory Committee could be effective.

An example of how important teacher pay was demonstrated in Fresno, California's school district. A teachers salary was agreed upon in 2001—a 3.98 percent raise. The reason given for non-payment of this agreement was "the district can't afford it." But at the same time the district and school board agreed to spend close to $200,000 to release the contract of a high-ranking administrator who had left for a better job. Guess how the teachers feel about this broad slap in the pocketbook?. Unfortunately it is not uncommon. See The *California Educator*, November 2001.

Quality Teaching: Many states require "Practice Teaching," which includes a semester or less working in a classroom with an experienced teacher at the grade level (elementary or secondary) specified by the credential. In my first practice teaching experience in a junior high, the regular teacher introduced me to his class, and then disappeared to work in his schools photo lab, leaving me to mangle the seventh grade English class. Fortunately for me, the kids were a very kind group. The only adult who came in to supervise me was my "practice teaching" professor who spent ten minutes in the class, and then left after correcting me on the use of "a" and "an."

The kids in this class were very concerned that I would give a bad time to an Hispanic boy who often slept during class sessions. He had just been released from juvenile hall for taking part in the robbery of a filling station only a block from the school. When he slept, the room was orderly and quiet. The kids didn't want to disturb him. When he was awake, I had my hands full. I'd like to say I cured him, but he was back in juvenile hall two months later.

The major criticism in teacher quality appears to be a lack of knowledge of what is being taught. The remedy is to have teachers acquire a deeper understanding of their subject matter — just as the major discussion about students is their failure on international testing. We seemed to be concerned with data, and not the understanding of how to help children learn, how to create an interest in a subject, and how to recognize the student's abilities, weaknesses, and interests. We want teachers who can pour data into the student's head from a pitcher, when we really need teachers who are sensitive to children's needs, weaknesses, and desires.

As Aristotle said, "Learning is not filling a vessel. It is kindling a fire."

A very knowledgeable teacher who taught in the room next to mine was highly proficient in biology, but she was not well-liked by most of the students and even the faculty. She came across as a tyrant who expected perfection from each student regardless of interest in the subject matter. Most of the students in the course were in a college-prep program and needed the credit, but less than half of the students passed her course with better than a C. Her basic problems were: poor social skills, no sense of humor, a vengeful personality, age 42 and single. None of us on the faculty were socially active with her or even knew where she lived. Still, she had met all the requirements for teacher-testing, and more.

In contrast, another teacher who taught handicapped sixth-graders was very positive, but with structure in the class; the kids knew what to do, when, and where to do it, and the consequences if they didn't. They knew the rules and helped make most of them. The teacher was very loving, a nice person to know, and friendly with the children. She said complimentary things to and about them on a regular basis. While maintaining excellent control in the class, she kept the students interested, met their needs, and had other children help explain what another student was supposed to do and know, adding to communication among the students and teacher. There *are* good teachers.

On my teacher rating scale, student test scores would rate about fifth on the qualities I'd like to see. My top priority would be the art of getting along with children, regardless of age, ethnicity, nationality and language. Second would be an interest in helping the children learn, for their interests, not for the teacher's. Third would be a deep concern for promoting positive self esteem and eliminating failure and degradation. Fourth would be a positive sense of humor, unlike one teacher. When asked by a student, "Do we have to do this homework?" replied. "Of course not. You don't have to do this home work. You don't have to pass this course. You can take it again next year! Ha, ha, ha."

Effective teaching: The theories of Piaget, Vygotsky and Erickson are strong on Developmentally Appropriate Practice that suggests children learn primarily through their own initiative. These long held theories involve: the teacher facilitating learning by interacting with the children following the goals of the children, rather than the teacher's goal or interest; the teacher helping the learner in self discovery and in activities of the child's choosing rather than those that are teacher directed. This self chosen activity should involve play in younger children, considered the most important activity for learning; children should work in mixed ability groups, non-graded, and non-age groups. Assessment should be based on observation and the child's evaluation of what has been accomplished, plus a description of further progress in that learning area.

William Glasser, the author of *Quality Schools,* was against assigning required subject matter, homework, and specific methods of learning and behavior. His main theme was that *The child must be directly connected to what is learned, and the teacher's primary function is to work toward improving the child's self concept by involving the student in the learning process and making the student successful.*

A problem mentioned earlier, however, involves teachers in difficult-to-teach classes. Very often new teachers are assigned to the most difficult classes, and are stuck there until the next new teacher comes along. Those teachers who take these difficult classes should have special training, reimbursement and rewards, just as special education teachers in many schools now receive. They should also be recipients of peer review from a variety of resources. Teaching is a profession that is poorly paid with little status in the community. With peer review and special help for teachers having difficulty and quality pay, this status might be improved.

Students Who Learn Differently

With good discipline, it is always possible to pump into the minds of a class a certain quantity of inert knowledge. You take a text book and make them learn it. So far, so good. The child then knows how to solve a quadratic equation. But what is the point of teaching a child to solve a quadratic equation? There is a traditional answer to this question. It runs thus: The mind is an instrument, you first sharpen it, and then use it; the acquisition of the power of solving a quadratic equation is part of the process of sharpening the mind. Now there is just enough truth in this answer to have made it live through the ages. But for all its half-truth . . . I have no hesitation in denouncing it as one of the most fatal, erroneous, and dangerous conceptions ever introduced into the theory of education. The mind is never passive; it is in perpetual activity, delicate, receptive, responsive to stimulus. You cannot postpone its life until you have sharpened it.

Alfred North Whitehead, *Education and the Good Life*, 1925

Imagine an authority figure — tall, mean, male, and frowning — telling you in front of a number of important people, "You are an 'I.T.'—an Irrational Thinker, and you will no longer be allowed to eat at this table. There is a special one for you over there." Similar ego-demeaning insults happen in our schools every day when we label children as learning disabled (LD), emotionally disturbed (ED), emotional behavior disorder (EBD) and other slanderous names and initials. Almost any child would respond to this with battered dignity, resentment, and despair. When the classifications first came out in the early in the 1900's, the terms "moron," "idiot" and "retarded" were used. While the terms are less demeaning today, the children still know who is labeled and who isn't, who is in a special ed. class and who isn't.

When children start school they generally believe that ability and effort are the same; that if they work hard, they'll become smart. Soon, however, they find that lower ability requires harder work, and higher ability requires less work. As a result, some children learn that working hard just isn't going to make it for them. They see academic obstacles as insurmountable, and devote less effort to learning. The most serious damage is to self concept. This should never happen to any child.

The reply from educators would stress the needs of children who have various kinds of learning problems and require special help. But what is the result of that "special help" for the majority of children so labeled? The data showing the effectiveness of special ed programs over a long period of time should be available showing success in self esteem, graduation, and employment or further education. The tracking, or placing children in special classes, while helping a very few stigmatizes most and seldom accomplishes any significant long-term improvement.

Special Ed Students: If the goal of public education is to teach children, some more difficult than others, to meet graduation standards, the grade is F.

Before 1960 less than one million children in the US received special education, but today nearly 5.5 million receive special education services or about 12 percent of all children and it is still growing. The cost of these services is increasing daily. The reasons for learning problems in children run the gamut of school and psychiatric labels. A child's learning problem may be diagnosed as involving behavior problems, being emotionally disabled in various stages, having Tourettes or Downs Syndrome, autism, fetal alcohol syndrome, and a wide variety of other names and acronyms which have proliferated geometrically in the last five years. In nearly all states these students require special classes with specially trained teachers. They also require school psychological services and regular meetings by members of the school staff at Individual Educational Programs (IEP) meetings to determine if the student fits the format to receive special education. This involves an enormous amount of school time adding to the cost of the special education student's learning. We have a growing number of children who need special help in school and at home.

Referral to a special ed class seldom insures graduation or employment after leaving school. Research has shown this lack of success of special education classes to be true, but schools continue with this ineffective system of labeling children and placing them in special education situations in separate classrooms at a tremendous cost in time and money. Paperwork has increased until the major part of the IEP meetings consists of making sure all the forms are filled out correctly, and little is done about preventing or reducing the student's learning problem. An IEP meeting will usually have the child's parents, his teacher(s), a special ed teacher, the principal (sometimes), and the school psychologist who did much of the assessment. In some cases when the parents are not satisfied with the school, they will have an "advocate," a lawyer type, and the school will have a specialist from the district office. The assessment reports on the child's testing results are presented by the psychologist and special ed teacher, the teacher relates the student's positive and negative qualities in class, and the principal will throw in instances of misbehaviors that resulted in punitive action from the school. Many times the ego needs of the IEP members result in long presentations and endless hours when the meeting should never be more than an hour. A decision is made on whether the child "qualifies" for special ed or not. The parents' advocate quite often can swing the decision in the parents' favor; whether they would like their child in special ed or not.

Children know when we think they can't learn, and many quit trying. The damage to the student's self concept is devastating. Wouldn't it be wonderful if we devoted our time to improving learning without labeling, and instead of IEP meetings we spent all that talent and time in helping the child to be successful? The response from the school would be, "But that's what the IEP meeting does."

"Educating students identified as seriously emotionally disturbed is one of the most stressful, complex and difficult challenges facing public education today, and perhaps one of our greatest failures." The article by NASP pointed out that "unsound instructional and behavioral interactions in classrooms for students with EBD (emotional behavior disorder) were more the norm than exception." Instead, students often were under "the curriculum of control that appeared to emphasize containment rather than purposeful academic activity and productive social interaction." Overall, the schools' attempts to help alleviate the behavioral problems of special education students by labeling and placing them in special education class has not been successful. The price the children pay for this categorization and the price the community pays in school funds is a combination that should be examined in every school for the sake of the labeled children and the financial losses (2).

The US Department of Education enacted new standards requiring school districts to make mainstreaming a priority. As a result, schools are required to justify placing disabled students in a more restrictive special education class. Congress adopted the Individuals With Disabilities Education (IDEA) in 1975, which required public schools to integrate disabled children into regular classrooms "to the maximum extent appropriate." But many school districts have traditionally taken the reverse approach, automatically placing disabled kids in special ed classes.

Parents of a girl with Down Syndrome battled the school system and won after a long effort the right to place their daughter in a regular classroom. Mainstreaming will help her prepare for that future, they pointed out. Segregating these students in a "special" class, and then expecting them to function normally outside the class in every-day life often works against facing reality. The Down Syndrome girl while mainstreamed was not required to meet the same academic standards of regular students to complete middle school but still will graduate. After her victory in court, the district went out of its way to create a full-inclusion program. Seven other students with Down syndrome were fully mainstreamed in the district along with 12 autistic children.

In California there were 640,000 students in special education programs, and on average they spent 66% of the school day in regular classes according to the state Department of Education. On average, educating a disabled student costs $12,000 a year, double the amount of a regular pupil. "The higher you go in the school district, the more they look at it as a matter of dollars and cents," said the mother of the Down Syndrome girl. The parents of disabled children also run into

75

teachers of the "old school" mentality who believe students with Down syndrome can't be taught. Unfortunately, the parents must fight the system, since if they leave it up to the school district, they aren't going to get much of an education for their child. The district's director of pupil services pointed out there has been a nationwide movement to main-stream special needs students, at least for part of the day, since the latest research shows that it is difficult to teach skills to severely handicapped students in isolation.

Special Ed; Legal Problems: The special education legislation jump-started in 1975 with Public Law 94-142, the *Education for all Handicapped Children Act* enacted in 1970 and not funded for five years. It has increased in volume as the number of special education students has proliferated. PL 94-142 was followed by PL 99-547 in 1986 and later combined with *Individuals with Disabilities Education Act* (IDEA) as PL 105-17 in June of 1997. Teachers and special ed. personnel are now forced to attend regular conferences to keep up on the latest rules and regulations, special education language and other changes. It is time-consuming, expensive, and detracts from the services that could be provided by these special personnel to help children learn and succeed in school. As a result, many school districts are unable to fully accommodate the needs of some special ed students, and the districts are placed in legal jeopardy by state and federal organizations after extensive investigations.

A few parents manipulate their children in order to receive a label so that they can get money from increased Supplemental Security Income (SSI). As was pointed out in court, the standards for defining a disabled child are subjective and ill defined. Some parents play the system by allowing their children to misbehave in school or letting them skip school and do poorly just to collect the SSI income. The payoff beats the AFDC (Aid to Families with Dependent Children) and parents are motivated to qualify their children as disabled.

Regulation Violations: The federal government is cracking down on the states in an effort to reduce the mismanagement of the special education programs due to overwhelming regulations and a shortage of qualified personnel. For example, one school district was under the gun for claims of mismanagement of its $93 million dollar special education program. Six years previously the system came under the federal gun due to inadequate services to over 12,000 special ed. students. What the system did that the Department of Education objected to was to place the students in regular classrooms, but without the support for the special needs they required. After checking the situation for over two months, the inspectors gave notice that unless the city conformed to state and federal special-education guidelines, the money for the program would be withdrawn.

An investigation in 1997 by the California Department of Education (CDE) and Office of Civil Rights (OCR) investigations disclosed the following information. The 1991-92 Coordinated Compliance Review report indicated a number of areas the district missed in dealing with special education referrals:

- The assessment of the student and the Individual Education Program (IEP) referrals were not completed within the required 50 days;
- The IEP's were incomplete and also contained "infractions."
- Some caseloads were "excessive," and assessment sometimes was not done in the primary language of the student.
- Prohibited tests, which could be any type of test that could be called an IQ test, were administered to African American pupils.
- Information on the IEP was incomplete along with excessive resource specialists' caseloads, and more.

Although each special ed. student is required to be re-evaluated every three years, approximately 1,400 did not meet this deadline. The psychologists available to perform the assessment were extremely overloaded, and the school board cut the funds to support special education. As a result, the committee required the district to develop a plan of activities to inform parents of their rights under applicable laws, inform staff of the requirements of the law, respond to parent and staff inquiries concerning services to students with disabilities, assist parents in requesting IEP team meetings, filing for due process hearings, and mediate the resolution of issues in filing complaints. The affect on the school personnel from these mandates was not positive.

Part of the problem was the placement of special ed. students in the regular classroom for either all or part of the day. Trained special education teachers are supposed to be available to help the classroom teacher with the added teaching problems, but in nearly all the cases, the help was not there. The educational program for these special ed students was often provided in writing by the special resource personnel or psychologists, and then was totally ignored by the classroom teacher who didn't have either the time or talent to teach separate programs to one or two special ed students in the class. As a result the children, instead of improving, grew worse in educational performance, and to the parents and special ed personnel, this became quite apparent at the next IEP meeting when the test scores and observations were reported.

This re-examination of the school district's efficiency record was brought about by a concerned committee *of parents* who notified the California Department of Education (CDE) of the major problems of their school district. This is an excellent example of how parent committees can make major improvements in the school by examining where the schools are meeting the requirements and where they aren't.

Special Ed. "Lawyers": At the present time service for the handicapped has changed into an enormously costly program for the schools. Parents in some states are now being advised and represented by "advocates," or lawyer-types with no required credential of any kind, who charge a fee to provide the parents with services at the IEP meetings and subsequent hearings. One advocate I've dealt with at several IEP meetings charged an up-front fee of $1,500 just for taking the "case," and $100 per hour for services. Often the fee is paid by the school when something is shown that the school did wrong, such as not having the test results in before a 50-day time limit, or not doing proper assessment, or declaring the child had no learning disability when somebody else said the child did. This legal attack on the school system has escalated across the US with the potential for further depleting meager school funds, which will continue to divert money from schools with lesser funds. While most parents may be very sincere about their concern for the quality of services in special education their child might receive, at times their concern smells like blackmail. One executive said, "You'll just have to give parents whatever they want to avoid a lawsuit." Many schools are doing just that. It's cheaper to settle than fight.

One case involved a girl whose parents came to the IEP meeting with a lawyer. Their goal was to get the school district to pay the cost of the private school the girl had recently attended and liked. Because of the $9,000 cost per year of the private school the parents wanted to avoid, she was sent to public school. The IEP resulted in a hearing, and the case was decided in the parents' favor. The ruling stated the public school wasn't teaching her because the girl didn't try to learn in the public school the way she had tried hard in the private school.

In a similar case, an appeals court sent a boy to a private academy at a cost to the public school of $23,000 a year plus $13,000 for the boy's transportation, private psychological counseling and physical therapy. Another example concerned a group of children considered totally disabled, autistic and seriously retarded, who were flown on Monday to an institution that could "help" them, and flown back on Friday at a cost to the school of $4,000 per child per week. These cases are increasing.

Many medically disabled children are now attending public schools, and teachers are expected to perform medical procedures including track suctioning, tube feeding, catheterization, monitoring ventilators and administering oxygen among other medical problems. Under existing law, school personnel trained in the administration of these procedures can perform the services under the supervision of a school nurse, public health nurse or licensed physician. But with only one school nurse responsible for several school sites, supervision takes on a new meaning.

One response came from a teacher who complained that they were not trained as medical personnel, and while these children have every right in the classroom, the instructional staff should not have to perform medical procedures. But in the past, special ed students, particularly those with medical problems and multi-handicapped, have been more or less ignored, because teachers and others feel they have insurmountable problems that are beyond cure. The primary problem, however, is that these children need to learn social growth which doesn't occur in isolated classes. Children with disabilities do have feelings and need dignity and worth. The teachers lack experience with children of this type which leaves teachers with a serious problem in enhancing the child's social and emotional growth.

The Supreme Court ruled in March 1999 disabled children were entitled to public school education. The court decision upholds the 1975 Individuals with Disabilities Education Act (IDEA), which requires a "free and appropriate education" for children with special needs. While the decision opens the doors of public education to all students, it also places an enormous burden on schools that are in the lower income areas. With this decision, no child can be denied an education just because it is inconvenient or expensive for the school district to provide one. The cost will be enormous. For a 16-year old boy paralyzed from the neck down who requires daily health care including urinary catheterization, suctioning of his tracheotomy tube, feeding him, monitoring his blood pressure and the alarms on his ventilator, and making sure he's properly positioned in his wheel chair, the cost could run as high as $40,000 per year. The National School Boards Association estimates it will cost $500 million a year to provide individual care for the 17,000 students with medical problems attending schools in America—as much as $40,000 to $60,000 a year per child.

A twist in the financing came from the federal governments' refusal to pay the 40 percent of the cost of special education. The 1975 law upheld by the Supreme Court stipulated that the federal government would pay that 40 percent, but until 1995, the federal government avoided paying more than 5 percent of the cost of special education. In a recent year, $4.3 billion was spent by the federal government on special education. This is truly a crime by our Congress. California schools pay about $1 billion of the roughly $3.7 billion spent on special education yearly. The cost average per student was about $5,500 and has been rising about 7 percent a year. From 1987 to 1996 the number of special ed children grew 34 percent in California and 25 percent nationally.

The problem with special ed children, and particularly those who are disabled physically, is one that needs parental help immediately. While all the talk is going on about improving learning in schools, the federal government is ignoring the legal requirements of financial obligations due disabled special ed students. Why is our Congress unwilling to spend sufficient financial resources on learning? A PSAC group should investigate this failure to obey the law by our Federal government.

To show how the Congress works, in 1999 the House and Senate voted "not to authorize funds to hire 100,000 new teachers to reduce class size nationwide. Instead the Senate approved Senator Trent Lott's amendment allowing class-size funding to be diverted to special education." Bob Chase, the NEA president, said, "The Senate is asking America's schools to make a false choice between smaller class sizes and special education. In fact, both are priorities and both need additional funding in order to best serve our students."

If enough parents put the pressure on their congressional representatives, the change could be made, but it is patently obvious that our Congress will save money by underfunding our school system in a variety of ways, all of which reduce the learning level of students in low income schools. When there is a great deal of discussion about how to spend the federal budget surplus, the Republicans want to reduce the income tax amount, while the Democrats talk about reducing health care costs and protecting social security. Where are the voices for increasing school spending to produce educated graduates in all economic levels?

Another problem that worries teachers in these special ed classes with disabled children who require special nursing care is what happens if an emergency arises with a disabled student and the teacher makes a mistake? Will they be held legally responsible? The answer is, most likely, yes. Even the nurse who should be in the room, could be held responsible for risky problems. See Appendix B for more information on IDEA '97. The real tragedy about our categorization of children is that some, when taken out of the special classes, have improved dramatically. On the other hand, once the special ed. label is accepted by the children, their parent(s), and peers, progress slows down and self concept diminishes.

As one who has worked over two decades with this population of children, I am very much aware that in many cases the labeling process is unfair, destroys self concept, is ineffective in promoting graduation and employment, and must be changed until it proves successful. As the severity of problems escalates within the special education student population, teachers trained in dealing successfully with these students are decreasing in ability and numbers.

As special education teachers leave the classrooms, qualified replacements are very difficult to find. Many certificated special education teachers leave the field within the first five years. Statewide in California nearly 25 percent already have left. The school pyscholgists' job is overwhelming much of the time due to an abundance of cases and the lack of qualified psychologists to handle them. An overwhelming number of special education wavers resulted in order to fill the need of special ed teachers. Approximately 62,000 special education students are in classes with teachers not fully qualified for their jobs. According to California data, nearly every child considered for special education services ends up in a special education classroom. Categorizing students must be replaced by meeting the needs of each child by understanding the student's needs and abilities, the interests areas, strengths and weaknesses, and the student's long-term goals.

Illiteracy

If the goal of public education is to teach adequate reading skills to every child, American schools have earned an F.

The National Institute of Health reported, "Reading problems affect as many as eight million children between the ages of four and 13, with an additional 800,000 poor readers diagnosed every year." If these problems are not corrected by age nine, "a reading problem will become a lifetime struggle. People diagnosed as poor readers in elementary school often still have not caught up on their reading skills many years later," as evidenced from new research by Harvard University scientists. Often the failure of their teachers to teach them how to read leads to the label "learning disabled," and the child is shunted off to the special education class that most often is ineffective. With great regularity I have seen children with reading difficulties in the third grade placed in special education classes; the first step in low self esteem and treating reading as a difficult, if not impossible, task. When reading becomes a difficult chore, learning by reading is avoided. Parents should work with their children to set

14217-PIER

expectations and reinforce progress. School teachers and administrators should set specific plans of action to ensure that every child has mastered structured reading instruction.

Some Data:

Top and bottom percentage of students who were proficient readers:

State	1992	1994	1998
TOP			
Connecticut	34	38	46
New Hampshire	38	36	38
Montana	—	35	37
Massachusetts	36	36	37
Maine	36	41	36
BOTTOM			
Nevada	—	—	21
California	19	18	20
Louisiana	15	15	19
Mississippi	14	18	18
Hawaii	17	19	17

National Center for Educational Statistics

California recently ranked second to last among 39 states in a new federal assessment of fourth-grade reading skills. Only 20 percent of fourth graders were considered proficient readers. One of the reasons given was California's tendency to "embrace fads," based primarily on the state's battle over "the whole language" program and "phonics."

We have another reading problem: those who *can* read but who don't exercise this skill. More than 85% of US families have a tape recorder and many have a VCR and/or CD players. Books and movies on tape are common, and we now hear statements like, "The best book I ever heard." A two-year study by the Education Department, "Becoming a Nation of Readers" presented by former Education Secretary William Bennet, found children spending two to three hours a day watching TV and just a few minutes reading. In order to correct this problem, reading must be made interesting for young children. With the proliferation of senseless TV programs and increasing visual saturation, reading will continue to decrease as a sought after skill. Adult or parent reading to very young children on a regular basis is a very good start.

Deteriorating Democracy

If the goal of the public schools is to provide every student with an understanding and appreciation of our democratic system and to encourage involvement as a concerned citizen within that system, the grade is F.

Knowledge will forever govern ignorance; and a people who mean to be their own governors must arm themselves with the power which knowledge gives. James Madison, 1751-1836, letter to Lieutenant Governor Barry of Kentucky, August 4, 1822.

"Everyone who goes through our schools and the lesson they learn — not from what they are formally taught, but from the way the institution is organized to treat them — is that authority is more important then liberty, and discipline a higher value than individual oppression. This is a lesson which is inappropriate to a free society — and certainly inappropriate to its schools." Ira Glasser, "Schools for Scandal: The Bill of Rights and Public Education" *Phi Delta Kappan,* Dec. 1969, p 190.

When the data are examined as to who votes and who doesn't, those who are most recently out of high school have the worst voting record. The ages 18 to 24 have the lowest elector participation by far with a consistent decline over the past five presidential elections. In 1968 the 18-to 24-year olds had a 50.4% voting record; by 1984 it had dropped to 40.8%. A national survey of first-year college students found only one in four keep up with politics. The Higher Education Research Institute at UCLA's Graduate School of Education and Information Studies found less than 27 percent who said it was important to keep up-to-date with politics compared with 29 percent in 1996 — a presidential election year. When college students fail to exercise the voting duty, it is quite likely that others their age will be even more reluctant to learn about candidates and ballot issues.

The amount of votes cast of the total possible in our elections from 1960 to 1996:

presidential year			presidential year			
1996	49.0%	1994 38.8%	1976	53.5%	1978	37.8%
1992	55.2%	1990 50.1%	1972	55.2%	1974	38.8%
1988	36.4%	1986 53.1%	1968	60.9%	1970	46.8%
1984	40.1%	1982 52.6%	1964	61.9%	1966	48.6%

In 1998 only 38 percent of the eligible voters exercised their franchise.

It is exceedingly ironic that one of the fundamental reasons for public schooling is the transmittal of our national heritage, which usually translates as indoctrinating our students with national zeal and democratic principles as exemplified by our "founding fathers." What really happens is an apathy for democracy, and in most cases a complete ignorance of what it means, both in principle and in practice.

"Most high school seniors don't know enough about government and history to be responsible citizens," according to the Education Department's 1988 test of students in the fourth, eighth, and 12th grades. Just half the students knew that the US is a representative democracy; only 38 percent knew that Congress makes the laws, and almost 25 percent thought the president was permitted to break the law. About 32 percent of the high school students tested did not know the reason for the Bill of Rights. The study indicated white students performed much better on the tests than did Afro American or Hispanic students, with few familiar with the most basic US symbols and traditions such as the Statue of Liberty, July 4, and what the stripes on the American flag represent—compared with 85 percent of the white students. The conclusions are clear: without increased knowledge of our democratic principles in our students, significant representation by informed citizens will continue to decline.

Evidence of citizen abdication of the electoral process emerged as the single most disturbing finding of a two-year study focusing on the role of citizens, candidates and the media during the 1988 presidential election. The Markle Commission on the Media and the Electorate, May 1990, called for the creation of an "American Citizens Foundation" funded by an income tax check-off system that would promote a national advertising campaign to re-awaken voter participation in presidential elections. Since 1960 when 62.8 percent of the voting-age population participated in the election between Richard Nixon and John F. Kennedy, the decline has continued. Eighteen years later, when the elder President Bush retained the White House for the Republican party, turnout had dropped to 50.1 percent. It has not improved to any extent today. W. J. Clinton became a second term president with less than half of the voters participating (49.8%). The Bush-Gore election raised the question of accurate vote counts.

In one of the districts where I recently worked, all the schools but one, the high school, had elaborate ceremonies for celebrating Halloween. The elementary schools had parades with children in costume, teachers dressed up as Bo Peep, Dracula, and ghouls with parents taking pictures. In the elementary schools these activities took half the day. The November elections which followed Halloween received very little attention outside of a few class discussions in the high school.

Democracy is not promoted in our schools. The authoritarian action dealt to students in the name of learning is a daily violation of their civil rights—think of Zero Tolerance, expulsion and suspension, all violating the students' constitutional rights. Some schools provide an education that brainwashes students (and parents) into accepting rules and regulations from appointed officials who give the student dictatorial orders that must be obeyed, or else! While I recognize the need for keeping guns, drugs, and other weapons out of school, the penalty without a hearing or trial imposed on our school children wouldn't stand a chance of being imposed on our adult population. Why isn't democracy practiced in our schools? Why can a child be expelled from school without a hearing? Should compulsory schooling be enforced in a democratic society?

Who Benefits?

Robert Reich, President Clinton's Secretary of Labor, described our economy as apartheid; a political process in which the wealthy purchase the government they want while the needs of the bottom 60 percent of the population are largely ignored. This, he says, threatens the very foundation of our democracy. But it isn't new. It has been going on for a long time, and its momentum is growing. Any move to squelch this apartheid is soon destroyed. Almost half of the potential electorate failed to vote for the president, and two-thirds failed to vote on important state and local offices. The lack of voting intensifies at low levels of income and education, so that families in the higher socio-economic levels are over-represented. Our democracy has become a government representing mainly the upper and middle class income groups including those over age 50, and does not represent those in the lower income groups and minorities.

As the voters give up, the corporations, trade groups, unions, and other special interests move in. In the first half of 1996 the special interests groups spent $400 million to influence the federal election. The American Medical Association spent $8.5 million; Phillip

Morris spent $11.3 million; the US Chamber of Commerce spent $7.5 million, General Motors $6.9 million, the Christian Coalition $5.9 million, General Electric $5.3 million, AT&T $4.3 million and on and on. If the lack of participation in our democratic process continues, the result will be a government similar to those in some South American countries in which lobbyists and political action committees (PAC's) put into power those who respond favorably to their wishes. In 1998, according to public records, over $193 million in soft money was contributed by special interests to both parties with the Republicans getting 60 percent. This is more than twice as much contributed than in 1994.

Special interest groups are spending more than ever trying to influence state lawmakers. The top 100 lobbying groups spent a record $293 million during the 1997-98 legislative period according to the secretary of state's office. The percentage who contribute to their lobbyists and representatives is now growing in strength and thus receiving special consideration. As Bill Honig, ex-chief of schools in California said some time ago, "If we don't communicate to youngsters why this democracy is important, we risk losing this system." California Senator Dianne Feinstein declined to run for governor in 1998 with the comment, "Campaigns in California have deteriorated to such a point that there is very little uplifting or constructive about the process."

Since 1980 California has spent more than $8 million on locally directed voter outreach programs aimed specifically at the young, ethnic minorities and others with low voting rates. Registration continues to trail behind population growth. Belgium and other countries require citizens to vote or face a penalty.

An increasing election slogan is, " Vote early, vote often." Motor-voter registration has made it easier to cast fraudulent votes. Anyone can register to vote more than once or twice and more with no identification required. TV's 60 Minutes program reported a large percent of California's votes were from false voters. Bounty hunters, they said, get $5 to $12 per phony vote. They added, "The state requires a license for a dog, but you can register your dog to vote."

California has a state law effective 1 January 1997 that requires all public school students to read: the Declaration of Independence, the Constitution, the Federalist Papers, the Emancipation Proclamation, the Gettysburg Address and Washington's farewell address. How many voters have read these, and how many of the California state legislators who created this law could tell the voters what each required tract reveals? If skilled teachers could interest the students in reading these documents to find out how they affected voters in those days, the growth of our nation, or some other personal inquiry of the student, then it might have an effect other than providing more disregard for democracy.

Joseph de Maistre said, "Every nation has the government it deserves." Do we?

School Segregation

On December 1, 1955, Rosa Parks, a black seamstress was arrested in Montgomery, Alabama, on a city bus for refusing to give up her seat to a white man.

In 1948 blacks were granted the right to vote.

The case of Brown v. Board of Education 40-some years ago appeared to abolish school desegregation, but in actuality didn't come close. While this piece of legislation became law, a great many schools remain segregated, especially in the North and West. Schools continue to be nearly as segregated today as they were before this legislation. The law may have had an effect in the South, once the seat of segregation since it now has the highest percentage of integrated schools, but the trend has not expanded nationwide. Education Secretary Richard Riley when asked, how does school segregation affect learning, replied, "The vestiges of segregation are not just physical placement of people, but it's the quality of education itself." Robert

L. Carter, a NAACP lawyer who argued the Brown case before the courts stated, "More black children are in all or virtually all black schools today than in 1954."

Racism not only instituted the blatant number of blacks being placed in special ed. classes, as was pointed out in the Larry P. case in California, it is also seen in test results to place black children and other minorities in lower reading groups. As the result of testing, minorities are placed in inferior positions in schools where the rest of the class knows they are reading at a lower level and are not considered as smart as the rest. The inferior label is there for all to see — and is often accepted by the minorities themselves.

The federal court in the District of Columbia recognized this in Hobson v Hansen in 1967. The court wrote, "As a general rule, in those schools with a significant number of white and Negro students, a higher proportion of Negroes will go into Special Academic educationally mentally retarded (EMR) tracks than will white students." Today in California, blacks may not be tested with any exam that sounds or looks like an IQ test — even if the parents want their child to be tested— unless the parents state the child's ethnicity as something other than black.

One of the court findings revealed that reliance on group measures contributed to the mis-classification of approximately 820 out of 1272 students (64%). Evidence of mis-classification was provided by the school system itself. The court's major concern was not the tests, but inflexible ability grouping, the tracking system's stigmatizing effect on blacks, and its failure to provide sufficient resources to students in the lower tracks. The school system was asked to explain why blacks (and poor children) disproportionately populated the lower tracks. They couldn't.

To show how this bias works, Thomas Oakland in his book, *Nonbiased Assessment,* reported that in the early 1970's blacks constituted nine percent of California's population and 26 percent of the educationally mentally retarded (EMR) population in schools. Large numbers of minority group children have been routinely placed in the lower ability groups, EMR classes, and other administrative structures that are "ineffective and inferior to regular education programs."

Other efforts to "prove" the inferiority of blacks were shown by Steven Gould, a Harvard professor, in his book, *The Mismeasure of Man,* in which he discussed the fallibility of how we measure IQ. Gould explained how blacks were deemed to have inferior brains because of smaller skull capacity. F. J. Gall would take the skulls of deceased persons he wished to measure, and stuff the skull with small BB shot and declare smaller skull size meant smaller brains. "Scientists first tried to prove blacks were intellectually inferior by showing their brain size was smaller by measuring skull capacity . . . craniometry." Gould, however, then listed many famous men who had relatively small brains such as Cromwell and Swift, and the man who fostered phrenology, Franz Josef Gall himself (4).

Many people, including teachers, would be quick to point out that the black problem is the result of lower IQ, lack of initiative and work ethic, a proneness to pregnancy, and the willingness of Afro American men to desert the family allowing women to collect welfare. What is ignored is that being a black child has become synonymous with being poor. Congress has documented that these children are twice as likely as whites to die in their first year, three times as likely to be poor, four times as likely not to live with either parent, and five times as likely to be on welfare. For black children born to a single parent, the poverty rate is 85.2 percent.

Today 23 percent of Afro American males between the ages of 18 to 25, about one out of four, will end up in jail. This is a higher percentage than will graduate from college, and has a direct bearing on lack of school success, inability to gain employment, and the conditions of poverty in which they live. The schools in Afro American neighborhoods are notoriously lacking in teacher and school quality and have the lowest graduation rates.

Most white teachers would deny a bias against black, Hispanics or others, but it exists. The lowered expectations for minorities, educators say, are manifested in different ways. Sometimes it's a case of benign neglect—teachers not taking the time to find out why students may have failed a particular test. Other times it's a case of not demanding enough from "disadvantaged" students because of misplaced sympathy. Instead of helping the students, many teachers lower their standards with empathy for a single mother with six kids. This bias in low expectations can result in stunted performances. It's not easy for teachers to acknowledge the possibility of racism, the subconscious belief that some students, African Americans and Latinos, are likely to have a difficult time with some subjects. It is always a pleasant surprise to find an Afro-American or Latino who does well on an IQ test. And then comes the realization that this is bias — all should be expected to do well — to assume differently is prejudicial.

English as a Second Language (ESL) or Limited English Proficiency (LEP): Our school population today includes students who enter our schools speaking Hmong, Farsi, Tagalog, Spanish, Yiddish, Arabic, Hebrew and many other languages, but have very limited skills in English. According to a March 1996 Census Report, about 10 percent of Americans, or about 24,557,000, were born in other countries. At least 31.8 million people in the US speak a language other than English. California has 8 million foreign born, or about one-quarter of its population. In some urban areas over one-third of the children going to school will not be speaking English. Massachusetts' exams for driver's licenses have a range of 24 different languages including Albanian, Finnish, Farsi, Turkish and Czech.

In 1990, researcher Christine Rossell surveyed studies in the field and found that 71 percent showed transitional bilingual education was no different from doing nothing at all for non-English-speaking children. Yet the $10 billion bilingual program has made few changes even with large amounts of money to create these changes. Money will continue to be spent on inefficient educational programs as the schools go broke. Some studies, however, show that Korean, Japanese and Russian-speaking immigrant children manage to learn English with stunning swiftness. Part of this is due to parental concern for the child's use of English, and for the child's success in school.

An example of this unconscious bias concerns students and others who speak English with an accent. The reaction to an accent is typical for many Americans who immediately think that an accent means less brain power, and they begin to talk louder and slower, as if there were a hearing problem. All teachers and school personnel should have regular courses in facing subconscious bias and plain bigotry. When, and if this occurred, the grades of students from other cultures, especially blacks and Hispanics, would improve immediately.

It will be very difficult to prevent racism from influencing school children because of the categorizing nature of schools, the nature of school itself as a competitive institution that grades children on the basis of white standards, and tests that give the advantage to whites. The difficult part of all of this is that it is accepted not only by the whites, but by nearly all of the minorities—except some who drop out. Maybe this will change now that Asians are beating the white children at their own school game with better test scores and better grades.

The children I have tested for special ed evaluations who are limited English speaking, all have a difficult time on our English oriented tests. While we do have some tests in Spanish, we don't in the other languages many of these children speak. So how valid is the testing?

We need parent committees to help Hispanics and other non-English speaking families find success in our schools, to help them determine what goals they would like for their children based on their cultural norms, and to help our schools show respect for those who stay with the school system until graduation — and after graduation in life satisfaction and employment. While the US is steadily heading into larger multi-cultures, we are doing very little in public schools to ensure successful learning for all groups. The One-Lesson-One-Language-Fits-All philosophy has proven to be both inappropriate and ineffective.

In 1995 in California the limited-English speaking students numbered 1,262,882 according to the California Department of Education. The projected figure for the year 2015 is more than twice that figure, or around 3,250,000. There are enough states with similar problems to lead to a national economic crisis in the near future. This should be a major concern for all of us, the business world in particular.

Some Data: The black population is the second largest group in the drop out rate, and non-school graduation category. The ethnic group that does not follow this pattern is the Asians whose US population has increased from 1 million in the 1960's to 8.5 million. Meantime the white population, non-Hispanic, is decreasing as a percentage of the school population.

The figures for the US show:		*But by the year 2050:*	
White — 73.6%	Black — 12%	White — 52.8%	Latino — 24.5%
Latino —10.2%	Asian — 3.3%	Black — 13.6%	Asian — 8.2%

The figures for Los Angeles:

Latino — 43.5%	White — 35.1%
Black — 9.9%	Asian — 11.4%

Census Bureau

Some Questions to Ask

1. What is your school's dropout rate today and for the past five years? Is there a pattern as to dropouts in ethnicity, gender, grade level, teacher or locale?

2. How does the school score on city, state and national tests? What is the comparison with other schools' scores? Who or what is the test-taking population? Check the validity and reliability data on the tests.

3. How many teachers are "qualified," and in what way — courses, degrees, experience, skills? How many are not certified? What's the male-female ratio? Try to find a student rating of teachers — whom do they think of as good and bad? Teacher pay? Start a move to increase teachers' pay to attract more qualified personnel.

4. How many class sizes are over 25? Who gets the big classes?

5. Are high school graduates able to find employment? What kind of employment?

6. What is the value of the school's diploma in job seeking?

7. Check out tracking. What is the criteria for placing a student in a special education class or a gifted class? Is it merely low test scores and/or teacher dislike of the student? Who attends the IEP meetings?

See Appendix A for more questions.

PART THREE

WHY SCHOOLS ARE FAILING

(external causes)

The game is called "Let's Pretend," and if its name were chiseled into the front of every school building in America, we would at least have an honest announcement of what takes place there. The game is based on a series of pretenses which include: Let's pretend that what bores you is important, and that the more you are bored, the more important it is; Let's pretend that there are certain things everyone must know, and that both the questions and answers about them have been fixed for all time; let's pretend that your intellectual competence can be judged on the basis of how well you play "Let's Pretend."

Neil Postman and Charles Weingartner, *TEACHING AS A SUBVERSIVE ACTIVITY* 1968

Schools are failing for a variety of reasons. This section examines the external causes: those reasons outside of the school system that contribute significantly to the decline of our public schools. In general, these causes of decline are well known, recognized by the majority of educators, but little is being done to alleviate the problem areas.

It is readily apparent that unless some energetic efforts are made to improve the school system, the conditions listed in this section will continue to contribute to the further decline of American public schools.

The Pregnant Teenager and Single Parent

A federally sponsored survey of more than 17,000 children nationwide found that one in five under age 18 had a learning, emotional, behavioral or developmental problem attributed to the collapse of the two-parent family. By the time these children reach their teens, one in four suffers from malnutrition and social and emotional retardation. For male teenagers it is nearly one in three. Nicholas Zill, a psychologist and executive director of Child Trends Inc., a Washington-based organization that studied social changes affecting children, called it "the new morbidity of childhood," involving more than 10 million children. Emotional and behavioral problems were two-to-three times higher among children in single-parent homes or in families with one step-parent. Learning difficulties were nearly twice as high among children whose mothers had not completed high school as compared to those whose mothers had more than 12 years of education. Zill pointed out, "It is clear that learning problems tend to be tied in more with lack of intellectual stimulation of the children" (1). This is a major problem that requires national attention; not next year, but now.

The National Marriage Project at Rutgers University found that the percentage of high school girls who expected to stay married for life dropped from 68 percent in 1976 to 64 percent in 1995. Fifty-three percent said it was worthwhile to have a child out of wedlock, compared with 33 percent in 1976. The study cited the reason for this as the growing economic independence of women and the increasing number of children of divorce who are wary of marriage. The need for parental involvement in marriage and the family as a part of the school curriculum is an important concern that is seldom touched.

Having a child out of wedlock is no longer a sin, resulting from the independence of many single women in productive jobs, and children from divorced parents who no longer hold marriage as a virtue. This lack of parental concern is another major factor in the children's learning. As a result, a new fatherless family is becoming a regular part of American life resulting in children who are emotionally ill equipped to handle everyday problems. The quality of the home is a major factor, yet we as a nation continue to treat it as "none of our business."

"The USA has the highest teen-age pregnancy rate of any industrialized nation—10 times higher than Japan's and growing at 5% per year . . . Only 50% of sexually active teen-agers use contraception. In some ethnic groups, 80% of babies are born into poverty, and the high incidence of births out of wedlock has led to the collapse of the family unit." Most of the teen-age pregnancies are unintended. "Nine out of ten juvenile hall inmates are products of single-parent homes . . . The direct medical and indirect social costs of teen-age pregnancy approach $50 billion per year; the cost in shattered lives is incalculably higher" (2).

"I invite all Californians to join us in the Partnership for Responsible Parenting to reduce teen and unwed pregnancy. By working together, we can be the ones to make a difference," (Governor Pete Wilson).

Problems in Pregnancy: Unfortunately, the women at the highest risk for alcohol damage to the fetus have not eased up on drinking. Alcohol kills brain cells and disrupts normal migratory patterns in infant brain development. A study involving 400 people with FAS ages 3 to 51 found the most widespread secondary disability in 90 percent was mental health problems with children in school disrupting classes, fights on the playground, and in trouble with the law. Many ended up in juvenile hall or jail. Others could not live alone and were never taken care of by their mother. Alcohol and drug problems were common.

Recent studies show some improvement in the teen pregnancy problem. Statistics from Department of Health and Human services show that births to teenagers fell four percent in 1997. These data also included a record low number of births to unmarried black women and a continued decline in out-of-wedlock births in 1997. Nation wide, according to the sources, there were about 880,000 teen pregnancies in 1996 or about one out of ten teen females. Sixty-two percent involved 18-and 19-year olds with the other percentage in the 15 to 17 age range.

Scientists have known for years that smoking by pregnant women causes babies to be born smaller, sicker, at a higher risk of Sudden Infant Death Syndrome (SIDS) and, in some cases, even addicted to nicotine. A new study by the American Chemical Society in Boston offered the first direct evidence that fetuses of women who smoke actually metabolize cancer-causing agents contained in tobacco. Women with NNK smoked 5 to 25 cigarettes per day.

The ethnic group at disproportionate risk for tobacco use and illicit drug use is white, non-Hispanic women. In terms of the number of women exposed to substances, the tobacco and alcohol exposures are the most pressing statewide problem. Although the prevalence rates are relatively low, White non-Hispanic pregnant women are far more likely to test positive for amphetamines and methamphetamine than are women of any other ethnic group. *"These findings underscore the necessity for broad-based multicultural) prevention programs among adolescents to prevent initiation of smoking and alcohol use, and to warn adolescents and young women about fetal hazards posed by use of these substances."* Intensive effort is needed to warn pregnant women of these fatal hazards (3).

An example of FAS and the misery caused by maternal drinking sprees was exemplified in the case of a binge-drinking mother and her two children. The oldest son was retarded with brain damage and the youngest son suffered from mental problems. Instead of answering questions he would lick his lips, blink his eyes, and take a very long time to respond. He had some reading ability, but couldn't comprehend the reading material. The father was long gone. The mother when sober was a very nice person with a long-term alcohol problem. The young boy, however, had never been out of his neighborhood to a park or the beach. While the mother has apparently stopped drinking, the boys are disabled for life. This is a terrible consequence of maternal lack of knowledge of the consequences of alcohol consumption during pregnancy. Even though the mother is reformed, the lives of her two children have been permanently damaged. Shouldn't the mother be tried for child abuse? The defense, of course, would submit that she didn't do it on purpose.

Even larger sums of government funds will be spent dealing with this expanding school population in special education classes and residential institutions. These children need successful programs to help them lead a normal and productive life, which, at the present time, is not available to the vast majority of the children primarily due to poverty and lack of parental training in these skills. This training includes the important verbal skills that develop when the parent talks to the infant, the emotional understanding that comes from parental concern, and the social skills that develop from parental interaction with the child. Since it is highly unlikely that the governments (state and federal) will come to the aid of these children, the primary solution is the community's Parent-School Advisory Committee.

Chris, a secretary in one of the schools where I worked as a school psychologist, had raised six children, three boys and three girls, as a single parent. The oldest boy had just graduated from a university with a major in physics, and the oldest daughter was entering college. An eleven year-old daughter had been admitted into a gifted program. When I asked the mother how she kept the kids together without their father, she replied that she took them everywhere after school and on weekends. Her house-keeping suffered, she admitted, but the kids learned how to get along with one another. The older boys learned how to take care of the younger girls. Chris is proud of her family and stands as proof that not all single parents are failures.

Absent Fathers: About 38 percent of all children now live without their biological fathers. This is up from 17.5 percent in 1960. Fathers do make a difference with the child's achievement in school. A study by the Department of Education found fathers' participation in their children's schools helps the children's performance and slows down misbehaviors and academic failure. The children are less likely to repeat a grade and can get better marks, the study reported, when the father is present in the home. If both the mother and father were involved in the child's school work, about half were "A" students.

Legislation enacted had President Clinton's comment, "One way or the other, people who don't support their children will pay what they must." In one state the penalty included two years in prison plus fines for crossing state lines to evade child-support payments. Absent fathers are finding hiding has become a little more difficult. As a result of nearly 2.4 million active child support cases, the California Supreme Court has ruled that failure to pay child support is a crime. Many fathers have avoided getting a job to pay court-ordered child support, but now they either take care of their financial obligation or go to jail—sometimes.

Unequal School Funding

An idiosyncrasy in school funding finds that the richest one percent of taxpayers pay 5.8 percent of their income in school taxes, or 98 percent of school costs, according to the Citizens for Tax Justice. The bottom 20 percent in income pay 12.4 percent of their income for state and local school taxes. In general the children in poor rural

schools in Mississippi and Ohio had less than $4,000 for their educa-
tion per year, and school children in the South Bronx had less than
$7,000 while school children in the richest suburbs continued to
receive up to $18,000 yearly. These schools had the highest teachers'
salaries and attracted the most competent personnel; however, all of
these school children were held to the same national standards on
test scores to graduate.

Between 1960 and 1990, while student performance on tests such
as the SAT and the National Assessment of Educational Progress
(NAEP) dropped, inflation adjusted spending on K—12 public education rose from $50 billion to almost $190 billion. Per pupil spending more than tripled from $1,454 in 1960 to $4,622 in 1990 and is
still climbing.

Administrative Costs: One of the biggest inconsistencies in school
funding concerns the continual increase in the amount of money
spent for administrative costs despite decreasing enrollments. Why?
Non-instructional costs were consuming as much as 50 cents of every
school tax dollar in many public schools. The New York City Schools
was an example with less than a third of educational expenditures
actually reaching the classroom. In Milwaukee in one year a mere 26
cents of every dollar for elementary schools was spent on the kids.
Indianapolis schools fared only marginally better with 36 cents on
the dollar.

In California teachers had about 54 cents going towards classroom instruction, while the remaining amount went for maintenance,
transportation, administration, nurses and counselors. In California
private schools, the ratio of teachers to non-classroom personnel was
6 to 1 while in public schools it was 4 to 5. Until parents become
involved in school improvement committees, administrative costs will
continue to consume a disproportionate part of the school budget.

To pass a bond issue for public schooling, a two-thirds majority is
required in California which is difficult to achieve. The two-thirds

figure was voted in by home owners who pay the bond assessment via increased property taxes, and who didn't want a simple majority vote raising home owners' taxes. As a result, school bond issues suffer. But guess what sections of the community get the highest tax income for their schools—the middle and upper socio-economic status communities, while the lower, poverty areas get the least, and their schools show it. This is a major violation of "an equal opportunity" when it comes to an important issue — education. It's an appalling situation that should be corrected, particularly if we require all students to pass standardized exams for promotion from one grade to the next.

To bring the schools up to date in California it will require $42.5 billion dollars over the next ten years according to the California Department of Education. About $14.5 billion of this would go into new facilities for increased enrollment. The rest, $18.7 billion, would go to modernization and technology, $6 billion for deferred maintenance, $2.8 billion for permanent facilities for K-3 class size reductions, and $500 million for child-care facilities.

Increased School Spending—Funding & Test Scores: Educators argue that if we want to improve the public school, we've got to make more money available for financing good programs. The equation has always been, more money will produce better schools. SAT scores do not reflect that viewpoint. While there are those who question SAT scores and other test scores as a measure of quality education as I do, this is the accepted standard by the federal government and most educators: high test scores equal good schools. But some interesting data from Empower America and the American Exchange Legislative Council has shown that between the school years of 1972-73 and 1992-93 there was a 47 percent increase in spending for grades one through 12 in public schools. At the same time there was a 35-point drop in SAT scores.

Washington, DC, fifth in per pupil spending at $7,967 per pupil, ranked 49th in SAT scores and next to last in graduation rates. New Jersey had the highest per-pupil costs at $10,561 but ranked 39th in

SAT scores. Based on the importance given to SAT and other national tests, the investment doesn't produce the higher scores. As parents, we can make our schools economically sound by examining budget, staff changes and ratios of money spent compared with results, as well as changing the financial source of school funding—the property tax. If the money to support schools isn't applied equally to all schools, instead of giving the wealthier communities up-to-date schools, modern buildings, first class teachers, and all the wide variety of other advantages, then our society will continue primarily to turn out two distinct types of school students, graduates, low learners and drop-outs.

Legal Actions and Funding: The early 1970's legislation (Public Law 94-142 and subsequent enactments) provided families of children with learning problems assistance in getting the schools to provide services. Today schools are overwhelmed with the number of children referred for special education. Many schools do not have an adequate staff to handle the case loads, and often are forced to do a rapid assessment or go over the time limits allowed. More children each year are being classified as learning-disabled. The cost of special education is increasing daily as the legislation multiplies affecting definitions, assessment, plus new rules and regulations.

In some states parents can request their children be assessed for a particular problem — whether or not that problem really exists. The school psychologist is then required to assess the child within a certain time limit and provide the parents with the results of the assessment. This creates an overwhelming overload on school psychologists, since we are the only ones allowed to do the cognitive assessment as the funds for providing for additional school psychologists decreases. The daily function of school psychologists has steadily shifted from helping out individual students and teachers to doing assessment, write-ups, and attending the IEP meetings. In 1975 there were 800,000 public school students (1.8% of the total) classified as learning disabled; in 1998 the number was 2.6 million, or 4.3%. It costs $9 billion a year to educate learning disabled kids.

Under current law, a school principal or district superintendent may expel a student for drug possession. Current law also requires the district to continue educating expelled students in a different setting. These alternative settings cost more than regular school programs. According to estimates, approximately 17,000 students are caught each year possessing drugs at school or at a school sponsored activity off school grounds. The initiative mandates the expulsion away from school areas of students who unlawfully possess drugs at school or at school activities. The only exception to this requirement is a student's first offense for the possession of a small amount of marijuana. The cost? These mandates often result in additional state costs of $15,000,000 each year to educate expelled students. Additionally, there would be costs — in the millions of dollars — for districts to process expulsions cases as our schools go broke. If your school has this same policy, and very likely it does, find out what effect this program has on drug usage in the school or community. If there is no positive effect, it should be altered or dropped.

Business Funding Commercial interests are paying some school districts to allow them to provide the schools with programs in return for advertising. The reason given is that schools are desperate for money since the shortage of funds means less for capital improvements, library books, and other school essentials. The corporations also sponsor contests and incentive programs with prizes ranging from cash to free pizzas. The trade off is the contests carry brand names and logos into the classrooms. The demographic target many companies want to reach is the young people, since these 43 million students have tremendous buying power. Teens in particular have been noted for power spending, not only from their parents, but from their own earnings as well.

The rising interest in school-based marketing has spawned an entire industry of producers and distributors of in-school advertising and independent developers of sponsored educational materials that have as their primary purpose to get their message to school kids. Previously, the primary pathway markets to children were in the home with comic books, and television. Now it's the school.

Federal Funding: While the federal government has a budget for each state's educational allotments, that funding often does not make it from Washington, DC, to each state. Our congressional leaders were accused of dipping into money earmarked for school reform programs to finance perks for their home districts and to help well-connected constituents. This problem is not atypical of our elected officials who need the support from their constituencies for re-election. While they talked about improving our school system, lawmakers have used national education money to finance perks for their home districts, honored retired colleagues and helped well-connected constituents. Larding budgets with home-district projects is such a time-honored custom that it rarely gets little attention other than "thank you" from those who benefited.

The new trend is much more devastating due to the low amount of money for education. Over 90% of the Education Department's $33.1 billion annual budget is tied up in mandatory spending or money funneled to the states by formula. As a result less than $3 billion in discretionary funds each year is left for innovation, reform, research and investment. Congress ran out of time, and also gave in unwillingly to President Clinton's demand to spend $1.1 billion to reduce class sizes by hiring more teachers. But not before Congress rejected a nearly $1 billion school construction plan as a responsibility of local districts, not the federal government. Of course, the schools that will suffer the most are those in the most need; those in the low income areas.

This disregard by our elected representatives for addressing the issues in education needs concerned people in each state to keep tabs on their representatives who would reduce the spending for education in order to curry a favor from a potential donor. It just can't be taken for granted that educational funds enacted by Congress will reach their goal intact. Each school committee should have a representative to keep an eye on the state's school funding from both the federal and state governments. Our past history illustrates the need. Today, according to the General Accounting office, one-third of all schools are in need of extensive repair. This must be changed!

Violence

> A 14-year old right-handed girl with dark hair and baggy shorts with a good sense of humor said going shopping with her mother was one of her favorite things to do. Her father left when she was very young, but apparently still lives in the city. Her primary problem involved violent acts, threats to others, profanity, and suspensions. Retained in the sixth grade, she was placed in a special ed. class. She used profanity with the bus driver, and was suspended for "fighting, defiance, and threats to others." The reports also included truancy and non-attendance. She has been expelled from school twice this semester.

Over 400,000 Americans have been murdered since 1970—several times the number of Americans killed in the Vietnam War. In 2001 there were at least 500,000 more males in the dangerous age range, 15 to 19. Six percent of them will turn out to be violent criminals. The root cause of their alienation is the destruction of the family. These are the children who do not have two parents, and often only one parent who can teach them the positive survival methods in our society. Many come from single mothers, and others are raised by someone else. Their adaptive learning skills are limited and drugs and violent crime are not uncommon. Most of children's survival skills are learned prior to entering school. Children without these skills are the ones that need immediate help.

The US Department of Justice released the following figures on juvenile crime and violence in mid-1996:

- From 1988 to 1994 the arrest rate for children committing violent crime rose 50 percent.
- By 2010, if current trends continue, it will be double what it is today.
- The number of children murdered rose 82 percent from 1984 to 1994. Over half were ages 15—17. In 1994 the death rate for children killed was seven per day.
- Four times as many children used guns to kill in 1994 than in 1984.
- While blacks make up 15 percent of the juvenile population, 52 percent of the murdered children were black.
- Nearly half of all high school students knew of weapons in their school. About 40 percent said there were gangs in their school.
- About one quarter of violent crimes by youths occurs between two p.m. and six p.m. on school days. That's when many students get out of school, and the dropouts become active.
- In 1994, 35 percent of all children arrested were under age 15.
- Between 1985 and 1994 juvenile arrests for murder were up 150 percent, robbery up 57 percent, aggravated assault up 97 percent, simple assault up 144 percent and weapons-law violations up 103 percent. It has increased since then.

Today many children are afraid to go out of the house to play or even enjoy the parks in their neighborhood since they have either seen or heard from friends about the results of violence. They are aware that children in their neighborhood carry weapons including knives and guns.

When I asked a girl about what she would be doing at age 21 to help her plan ahead, she replied, "I'll probably be dead."

Violence is a major concern in our society affecting all our children. Community violence has reached epidemic proportions, and the United States is the most violent country in the industrialized world. Violence among youth ages 11—17 has increased 25% in the last decade. There are effective programs available to reduce violence. Check out *Hurt Healing Hope: Caring for Infants and Toddlers in Violent Environments,* ZERO TO THREE/National Center for Clinical Infant Programs, 2000 14th *Street North,* Suite 380, Arlington, VA 22201-2500, (703) 528-4300, fax (703) 528-6848.*).*

School Violence: President Reagan cited a 1978 report by the National Institute of Education (NIE): "Each month three million secondary children were victims of in-school crime. I don't mean ordinary hi-jinx, I mean crime. Each month, some two-and-a half million students were the victims of robberies and thefts, and more than 250,000 students suffered physical attacks." In large cities, the problem was so bad that almost eight percent of urban junior and senior high school students missed at least one day in the classroom per month because they were afraid to go to school. School violence has increased dramatically since President Reagan made this speech. Twenty percent of American middle schools and high schools reported at least one serious crime such as rape or robbery to police, according to the Education Department in March of 1998.

Child Abuse: The number of children abused and neglected rose to 2.81 million in 1993—up 98 percent from 1986 when the last report by the Department of Health and Human Services was issued. The number of seriously injured children nearly quadrupled in 1993. These statistics, the report indicated, appear to "Herald a true rise in the scope and severity of child abuse and neglect in the United States." Stress in the home often results in violence most often by the parents. The children of single parents have a greater risk of being harmed by physical abuse, by physical neglect, and suffering serious injury or harm from abuse or neglect over children living with both parents. This anxiety affect on children produces various forms of emotional problems that places learning far behind self protection and aggressive responses.

Domestic Violence: A warm family is the best defense a child can have against trauma, but all too often in cases of domestic violence that defense is absent. Many of the parents have had a similar background which makes sensitivity to their child's problems very blunted. Family therapy should be the primary goal since the trauma cannot be mastered until the family is stabilized and the parents feel safe. I found this to be the case in many families I counseled in which the father felt strict discipline, including physical punishment, was the best way to raise a young child, especially boys. It took a few sessions before the two parents' differing ideas on parenting could be blended with that of the child to use more practical methods of changing children's behavior other than fear and/or violence. It is patently evident many children need help in avoiding domestic violence. And more on how parents feel about children's behaviors—from past experience.

Overall: Much of the violent behavior has been attributed to the demoralizing violence on TV and in the movies with outrageous montages of blazing guns, exploding cars, and heads and bodies hurtling out of windows. The shattered glass and bodies look real enough to leave disturbing after-images. Then there are the bone crunching, bloodletting sports contests with videos of football's hardest hits, complete with spliced-grunts and groans. Also included are the plethora of fights, not only in hockey games, but on the basketball court and baseball diamond, and reels of race car crashes with flames, bodies, and metal. Fans seem to love them and they sell—the video games with extreme violence offered to children, (kicking, breaking bones, knockouts)—Mortal Kombat (with a "K" no less) advertises, "Wanna knock Sonya's block off or tear the spine right outta Kano?" Why is this permitted in a civilized society? We have rules against pornography; why not against the promotion of violence?

TV does influence violence. Studies have shown that a large percentage of children become aggressive, and more violent after watching violent TV programs. Younger children are affected more than older ones, and boys more than girls. There is more copying of the violent acts when the violence is considered a necessary part of the action or rewarded in the story, when it is demonstrated as painless, and when it shows the victim quickly recovering. Many children live in homes where the parent is absent much of the time, and they select their own violent entertainment. TV also has become the most convenient baby-sitter since Grandma.

Cures: Some cities have made welcome gains against the spreading crime rate. New York and Houston have reduced their crime rates with programs involving community-based policing strategies in conjunction with citizen anti-crime initiatives and continued target-hardening by private individuals and businesses that are beginning to show positive results. In Houston the Citizen Patrol Program operated in more than 100 city neighborhoods, reporting suspicious or criminal behavior ranging from assaults to drug dealing. Silverton, Oregon, and the Oregon legislature have passed legislation that holds parents responsible for offenses committed by their children but only up to the age of 15.

While violence is a major problem, with parental help we can reduce it.

Poverty — A major contributor to school failure.

If the misery of our poor be caused not by the laws of nature, but by our institutions, great is our sin.

Charles Darwin, *Voyage of the Beagle* 1946.

Children: The disparity between our rich and poor populations is presently growing at a steady rate, and this will continue due to the expanding economy, the downsizing of many corporations due to mergers, increased efficiency, and movement into our technological

113

age. Unemployment in the urban areas is affected by employers' disregard for the high school diploma from an urban school. The wages of the bottom three-fifths of our population have dropped since 1991 as a two-tier economy is created which consigns most of those without college degrees to menial service jobs, or no jobs at all. These are the students who live in a community with high rates of crime and drug dealing. They will be exposed to lead poisoning, poor diets and live in a family that is on welfare.

Our poverty rate is growing in spite of increases in our economy. The war, due to the assassination of thousands of innocent people in New York and the Pentagon, will further limit the funds for public schooling. We have a serious problem that will continue to deplete our schools and result in less funds for improvement.

The ramifications for this poverty problem are vividly evident in our schools and in our society. There were 13 million children with no health insurance, one-fourth of whom dropped out of school, plus thousands more who will continue to prove inadequate for the job market.

Studies have repeatedly shown that low income exerts a powerful impact on student achievement. Wealth is the strongest influence on test scores, and as the percentage of poor students increases, scores decline. As low income areas expand, the influx of these students into our school systems will increase, creating significant school problems since the majority of these children will not have the essential learning skills provided by their parent(s) during infancy and preschool years to enable them to be successful in school in terms of passing grades, graduation, and employment. This is a learning catastrophe that can be prevented if the parent is taught the skills that enable the "at risk" children to succeed in school: how to prevent pregnancy problems in infant development, and teaching the verbal, emotional and social skills in the child's early years that are largely ignored in low income, urban families due to a variety of reasons. At the present time, however, this population of "at risk" children is largely being ignored, while our school systems are requiring tests be passed at various grade levels for promotion and graduation.

There is always resistance to helping poverty families due to our Protestant work ethic which may have been valid fifty years ago. Today we have families who work, but do not make enough to rise out of the poverty area. There are many families with a full-time working parent unable to escape the poverty levels. Help is needed to keep these children from low income families in a healthy state of mind, eager and ready to learn with the same essential mental tools available to the upper SES children. The PSAC could make this a primary goal.

Middle Income Children: Infants and children from middle income parents are exposed to some of the problems faced by the lower SES families. The risk involves absent parents, both at work or a working single parent. This poor quality child-care places children at a greater risk than the two parent family. This pattern has developed slowly along the years with increasing numbers of children from middle income families unable to receive the necessary child care from the parent. Many of these children are raised in day care centers, with little, if any learning of important social and emotional skills.

The University of Colorado looked at 401 day care centers in California, Colorado, Connecticut, and North Carolina, and found that 91.5 percent of the day-care centers had mediocre to poor care for toddlers age two and under. The day-care providers seldom involved themselves in interactions with the children necessary for verbal, social and emotional growth. Seldom were the children picked up, talked to, or involved in play. When asked about the care-givers, the parents rated them as "OK" since their evaluation was based solely on baby-sitting rather than providing appropriate time for the child to learn and to grow. Many middle class parents will also need the help of the PSAC when their children come to school with inadequate verbal skills, and feelings of rejection from being placed in a day-care center on a daily basis.

The unfair treatment children in low income schools are receiving has been continuous over a long period of time. Milton Schwebel wrote about it in 1968 (5). A year earlier Edgar Z. Friedenberg pointed out that the school situation was almost hopeless in late 1967 because the cities had neither the budgets, the personnel, or facilities to cope with the accumulated problems caused by years of neglect (6).

Why does our nation, the most prosperous on earth, ignore the major problems in education in low income neighborhoods? Why isn't the goal to improve learning and reduce ignorance a goal of many organizations and especially religious ones? The cycle of poverty from one generation to the next doesn't have to be continuous. We can start with care during early pregnancy to help children have a normal, healthy birth followed with early childhood learning skills. Next would be equivalent school systems in both upper and lower income neighborhoods. Why aren't these a major goal of our society? The answer is obvious. This is why concerned parents must help reform our schools.

Drug Babies

After removal from the family for neglect by parents, both drug addicts, the girl lived in foster homes. A hospital had diagnosed her as dysthymic (depressive), oppositional defiant, and having an anti-social personality trait. She had been shuttled from one place to another because of assaultive behaviors, attacking staff members, slashing her wrists, and trying to swallow broken glass. During our session she was very friendly, complained about not seeing her parents for some years, and claimed she wanted to work in the zoo since she liked animals. She can't go home because she and her mother "come to blows," but later she asked, "How can I become emancipated?" She was living in a residential institution she disliked intensely.

Here is a brief look at a random sample of some students I worked with in the public schools. Each description could fit a very wide sample of students in schools then and today.

White, male age 17. Mother overdosed on drugs; father unknown. His brother, age 19, was in jail for selling drugs. The older brother started the younger brother on drugs at age eight.

White female, age 15. Abused by her mother, sexually abused by her father, early baby sitter and her stepfather. Neglected. Full Scale IQ = 112, good; also depressive, uses a variety of drugs.

White male, age 15. Father died when the boy was age one. He was sent to multiple foster homes. IQ = 102, depressive, self abuse, schizophrenic, hypervigilant, depressive, on drugs.

Black male, age 11. Placed in a class for children with a serious emotional disturbance in the first grade; negative, angry, schizophrenic, mother was on drugs, father dead.

"In March 26, 1990, the House of Representatives sent a letter to Leon Panetta, then the Budget Committee Chairman, stating: 1.) The first wave of 'drug babies' is about to hit the schools. According to a recent national study, 11% of newborns—375,000 babies each year—have been exposed to illegal drugs in utero. 2.) A recent study has shown that, due to medical advances, twice as many children are surviving severe birth defects into adulthood as did 25 years ago. They are entering the schools in growing numbers and at younger ages" (4).

A study in California indicated eleven percent of the pregnant women used alcohol and drugs while pregnant. Several California universities and the Western Consortium for Public Health in Berkeley found through urine analysis that a large number of pregnant women were using alcohol and other harmful drugs. Alcohol, drugs and tobacco during pregnancy can result in an infant who has low birth weight, FAS, and other neurological and physical problems. The number of children I deal with who have had drug using mothers before and after birth has steadily increased over the years. The effect is criminal, since the results of parental substance abuse destroys a meaningful life for many of the offspring. A court recently found a mother who ingested drugs during pregnancy guilty of child abuse.

These "drug babies" cause serious problems with behaviors that range from severely limited to totally unmanageable in school. They often are impossible to control in a classroom, while education and learning take a back seat to disciplinary techniques. Steps are being taken to curb or slow down the birth of such infants by charging the mother with a felony, but the odds of decreasing the number of infants born with drug problems are limited at best.

According to Public Law 94-142 and subsequent legislation, these children are entitled to an education, but in many cases it is at the expense of the education of other children. I have tested many of these children and worked with some, but I must admit, that for many, hope for improvement or positive change is extremely limited. There appears to be a neurological malfunction that leads to behaviors unthought of in normal children.

A mother in South Carolina was jailed recently because her newborn son tested positive for cocaine. Chief Justice William H. Rehnquist denied an emergency plea for an appeal. The state Supreme Court had ruled that a late-term fetus was covered by the traditional child endangerment law, but this woman had been drug free for three years after the child's birth, and her lawyers said this policy " . . . is destroying families and undermining children." An organization called PETA, People for Ethical Treatment of Animals protests the fur fashion craze that results in killing animals. How about a PETI, People for Ethical Treatment of Infants?

While there appears to be widespread concern about abortion, there is much less concern for children coming into this world with dysfunctional mental abilities due to the mother's drug and alcohol intake. Shouldn't there be laws in every state against this? If a man fathers a child, shouldn't there be much more attention given to his responsibilities? The father should be required not only to help care for the child, but to pay the expenses of normal, healthy prenatal medical care, as well as the costs of the birth. Those fathers who ignore these expenses should be tried and fined, if not sentenced. It should be common knowledge in every sector of our society that having an infant is a privilege that requires specific understanding of child development and financial expenses, which must be met by both parents before and after the child is born.

Some Data: The Department of Health and Human Services survey of 17,747 students revealed more than 2.4 million youths between the ages of 12 and 17 admitted using illicit drugs at least once during the previous month. Drug use among 12—17 year olds rose 105 percent from 1992 to 1995, or an increase from 5.3 percent to 10.9 percent involving 22.2 million Americans in that age group in 1995. Marijuana was the leader with an increase of 150 percent from 3.4 percent of teenagers using it in 1992 to 8.2 percent in 1995. The estimate is that in 1994 alone, 2.3 million people started using marijuana. Beer, wine and distilled spirits were also in the picture for those under age 21. The number from the study was 4.4 million described as "binge drinkers" along with 1.7 million called "heavy drinkers."

While drugs are still an issue, alcohol consumption by students is rarely mentioned, yet more than half of America's teen-agers consumed alcoholic beverages, and, according to the US Attorney General, most didn't have any clear information about what it was they were consuming.

Gael Edward Pierce

The White Flight

In 1970 one-third of Atlanta city's students were white. As more students moved to the suburbs, the schools became 91 percent black. In New Orleans black enrollment increased from 50 percent to 85 percent. Theodore Shaw of the NAACP Legal Defense Fund said the result of the tendency of whites leaving a district that gets over 25 percent minority is "resegregation in which city schools become blacker and poorer."

This exodus is partly the reflection of parental changes in values. It began with the preference of some parents to send their children to private schools. It increased when integration in schools became unpleasant to some parents who organized their own private schools so their children would not have to mix with minorities. A third impetus to the white flight came from those parents who were afraid of the low moral values and anti-Christian attitudes they believed existed in public schools. They opened their own private and religious schools and have continued in that mode. The people leaving the public schools, are generally the ones most interested in their child's education and possess the finances to look elsewhere. The White Flight depletes the public schools' source of income, the Average Daily Attendance (ADA).

Not only will decreased confidence in the local schools speed up the white flight, but vouchers and tax credits will lend further impetus. These funds will enable those parents who have the money to make a choice of schools, to use that option to send their children to private schools, and then be compensated in tax deductions or direct payments (vouchers). The low-income families will be forced to keep their children in the public schools as the school system becomes even less functional.

Home Schooling

All states allow home education in some form or other. Iowa and Michigan required the parents to have a teaching certificate, and, of course, the NEA supports this. Twenty other states require the passing of standardized tests, having a teacher "consultant," and other stipulations. California has the euphemistic term, "independent study," and home schooling has been in use for many years. Parents can declare their home a private school and fill out an affidavit showing everything from a curriculum to a health department inspection of their home, just as a commercial private school would. District programs furnish a credentialed teacher for every 30 students, and this teacher acts as a counselor to the parents. This also enables the district to count a percentage of home study students as part of their ADA. The parents get counseling, a curriculum, and a teacher's edition of the textbook. A minimum of four hours per day is recommended for instruction, plus workshops, field trips, and access to computers and libraries. While grades are seldom given to home study students, a diploma results from district credit in most cases. In 1996 California had ten thousand families with children doing most of their studying at home, and, according to some parents, it is not a simple matter. It involves a lot of work to educate at home. Some parents don't make it.

On the other hand, students in home schooling avoid the cut-and-dried public school format that enforced enrollment, dealing with information of no value to the student, avoiding lectures, homework, and tests produced by outsiders (in most cases).

In Summary

A general state education is a mere contrivance for molding people to be exactly like one another; and as the mold in which it casts them is that which pleases the predominate power of the government, whether this be a monarch, a priesthood, an aristocrat, or the majority of the existing and

successful, it establishes a despotism over the mind, leading
by natural tendency to one over the body. An education
established and controlled by the State should only exist, if it
exists at all, as one among competing experiments, carried
on for the purpose of example and stimulus, to keep the
others up to a certain standard of excellence.

John Stuart Mill, *On Liberty*, 1859.

It is apparent that the scenario for schools will not change substantially , unless parents can make some satisfactory changes in their
communities through the PSAC groups. We will see decreased funding for schools as more autonomy in schooling is left to the states —
even as our economy blossoms. This will increase the number of unqualified teachers as our student population grows. It will contribute
to a steady flight from public to private schools, more than doubling
the number of students in private school enrollments, as discipline
continues to be a pervasive concern.

As our economy continues to increase, the difference between
the affluent communities and the barely-making-it neighborhoods
will expand, and education commissions will prescribe more castor
oil remedies (if one spoonful doesn't work, take two). They will call
for increased hours, stricter academic requirements, better test scores,
more days in attendance, and try to catch and surpass foreign test
scores to accommodate the business interests. The dropout rate will
continue to increase until less than 50 percent of eligible students
are attending public schools. This will increase our prison population which has jumped from .7 million in 1985 to 1.7 million in 1996
at a staggering cost. And like schools, prisons fail to teach appropriate social and emotional skills for survival in our society. The more
successful students will be those in private schools either paid for by
vouchers or tax credits. The remaining 50 percent of students in the
schools will continue to receive the custodial care they now get. In
the meantime, our country will experience an influx of immigrants
with some qualifications to fill the growing number of job openings
that require certain educational levels.

There will be isolated pockets of good schools along with some minority and urban schools run by charismatic principals and others reformed by PSAC's. Minorities, at risk students, and non-English speaking children will continue to flow into the school systems in larger numbers, making teaching even more challenging and frustrating. Thus, any teacher who can do anything else for a living, will. Those who can't, and those few dedicated teachers, will remain aboard as the schools sink. Major programs suggested to reform schools may be tried in some areas, but, in general, schools will continue their monolithic, single mindedness with more concentration on coercion to learn information of little interest to the student to reach a goal the student doesn't really understand or sees as desirable — *unless parents become involved.*

Due to the suicidal bombings in New York in two different buildings and the Pentagon, our economy dropped due to airplane traffic problems, a severe reduction in passengers, and billions of dollars going in to help the airlines and others. This, no doubt, will decrease the funding for our schools since they often are on the lower end of the priority list. Our children's education will lag behind the shift in priorities to protection and revenge. PSAC will become even more important during this prominent period in our lives.

Some Questions to Ask

1. What is the ratio or number of teenage pregnancies in your community? What percent without the fathers present?
2. Check out the school funding for total income. How it is dispensed, to whom and when? What are the administrative costs, teachers' salaries, special education expenses, business interests in the school(s), state funding, and federal funding to the state? You need an understanding of how and where school funding is utilized. What percent goes into the classroom?

3. Is violence a major issue for children and parents—how severe and in what localities? —and what is being done to reduce it?

4. How large is the low income population and upper income school population — and what effect does that have on your school?

5. Are there data on drug use in your community? Are there successful programs being used to reduce drug usage?

6. How do teachers' salaries compare to equivalent jobs?

7. How much positive reinforcement is used in the classroom compared with negative reinforcement—punishment?

8. Make sure the parents of special education students are familiar with the school's program requirements for special education, and the state and federal qualifications that apply. Also, how much confidence is there in the school's special education personnel from teacher to psychologist?

9. Does the school meet the legal, state, and federal regulations and other qualifications for special education? Get the school psychologist to help you with this information.

10. What does the school psychologist do besides testing children?

See Appendix A for more information.

PART FOUR

Some Good Schools

I hear and I forget
I see, and I remember
I do, and I understand

Chinese Proverb

The fact itself, of causing the existence of a human being is
one of the most responsible actions in the run of human life.
To undertake this responsibility—to bestow a life which may
be either a curse or a blessing—unless the being on whom it
is to be bestowed will have at least the ordinary chances of a
desirable existence, is a crime against that being.

John Stuart Mill, *On Liberty*, 1859

Part Four deals with the characteristics of good schools, teaching
reform, and teaching techniques plus suggested changes in the curriculum and innovations. Some Questions to Ask completes the section.

The Basic School: What Your School Could Look Like:

In a Basic School there are no failures and the teachers stay with
the same children for three to four years. Retention has been eliminated. The main idea is that when children enjoy what they are learning, they feel successful. Each child learns differently. The teacher-

facilitator uses different learning styles in helping the children. In most schools, few teachers have training in alternative methods, but in the good schools, teachers have the autonomy to try different techniques. The children have a balance of freedom and responsibility. In a gradeless system, the children go as fast as they want with frustration eliminated, and older children helping the younger children. The Basic School allows flexibility and eliminates the yearly pass-fail fiasco. John Dewey many years ago suggested that schools should treat children as people and accept them as active participants in the school.

A Magnet School utilized what was called the "Micro Society;" an involvement of the students into a working community with its own money, a court system to try misbehavior, a discussion of taxes, and a debate of the values of each—the outside world in miniature. The students seemed to appreciate it as "real life" learning. Another school put students in apprenticeship programs to help them learn vocational skills, and to demonstrate to them that learning certain concepts (for example, fractions) related to the outside world, plus community involvement, important to learning how to adapt to social life, and participation in democratic functions.

One of the most important parts of the good schools was the goal of empowering the students. In almost every case, negative reinforcement was eliminated; that is, failure, humiliation, derogatory comments in front of the class, and in its place, respect for every student. Each child was expected to learn and make decisions concerning learning. The good schools exhibited an attitude toward children, as demonstrated by the teachers and principals, that regarded them as important persons. For example: award ceremonies were held at regular intervals to recognize good students, achievement, and progress. Positive reinforcement was a regular part of every classroom, and the teacher evaluations sent home stressed the positive side of the students' performance. The principals in the good schools learned the names of many students and talked to them frequently before and after school.

In one school a teacher listened to students protest about the heavy workload. She then ask the students to form a committee on the problem and come up with some recommendations. The committee recommended no more than thirty minutes of homework per night, and no more than one test per day at school. The teacher agreed and spent a lot of time with the other teachers working out a schedule to fit the agreement. As a result the students did even better. Class committees as part of the regular classroom procedure promote greater student interest and interaction. See the book *Positive Discipline in the Classroom* for more on class committees.

Teaching Reform

> "Education with inert ideas is not only useless, it is, above all things, harmful . . . The child should make (the main ideas) his own, and should understand their application here and now in the circumstances of his actual life. From the very beginning of his education, the child should experience the joy of discovery . . . No more deadly harm can be done to young minds than by depreciation of the present. The present contains all that there is. It is holy ground; for it is the past, and it is the future."
>
> Alfred North Whitehead, *The Aims of Education*, 1924

A successful teacher must know a great many personal characteristics of the child including learning style(s), self concept, long-term goals, family, and other information in order to provide learning in the student's interest area. When that occurs, meaningful learning takes place. Many people, such as E. D. Hirsch of educational fame, would argue that the child must be made interested in certain learning areas, and in some cases this may occur; that is, the child is forced to learn physics, and finds that there are very interesting areas that appeal. However, there are also many more students who find that forced learning can be avoided or circumvented. Learning is defined by the student first, then supplemented by the teacher. Anything different from that falls into the risk of forced knowledge which is taken in quickly and erased even quicker. As a school psychologist I am always dumbfounded to observe a class, which I do quite often, to see the teacher forcefully cramming a specific subject down a student's throat, and the child using various means to play-the-game without overt revolt.

An example of this is forcing students who fail a class or a grade to attend summer school. In the summer of 1997 in Chicago, 7,400 eighth grade students were forced to go to summer school or accept their failure and not enter high school. It was estimated that about 2,000 would not pass the summer course. Overall, about 150,000 students out of 420,000 (35%) were forced to attend summer school. What were the results? It doesn't take a wizard to figure it out. Why did the student flunk in the first place? Was it lack of ability? Poor teaching? Sickness? Getting even with parents? What causes led to the failure? What will make the student see the mistake and try harder in the summer when all the friends are having fun? The odds are high that the dropout rate will increase as some students may have the desire and enroll in summer school, but then quit when the going gets tough again. Others will not even try since they've played the game earlier and lost. What is the reason for giving up a summer?

Checking Out Reform: Be very careful in evaluating school reform programs based on "vast research" unless that proposed program has been demonstrated by research to be effective in its main goal — not test scores, but by student interest and success as shown by graduation and employment data. If the parent committee does go for test scores, make sure the research is applicable to your school population, not data collected on a Peruvian tribe in the Andes Mountains. The data, for example on a reading program, should show the study was successful over a long period of time (several years), on a population that matches your school's students in age, language, culture and ability, and the techniques used can be applied to your student population. The reason for this, of course, is that there have been so many new programs tried in different schools simply because something different was desired, only to flop a year or two later.

An example was the effort in California to reduce class size in elementary schools to 20 students. It sounded like an excellent idea. After it was announced in Los Angeles and put into practice, enrollment increased nearly three percent—667,624 students. Many of the new students came from private schools with the parents obviously thinking smaller class size would promote better education and less expenses. Soon the schools were back to the crisis point with 77 of the 439 elementary schools new classrooms in former libraries, 30 in auditoriums, and 87 in other facilities including parent centers and child care rooms. Other schools divided the classroom among teachers with sometimes 40 students in one room with two teachers. The schools with room to accommodate downsizing classrooms to twenty students were in the upper income areas; the low income area schools were already overcrowded. To add to the problem, the teachers then demanded that other classes be down-sized.

All this has led to the need for teachers with a significant drop in experience levels due to the extra classrooms. In 1997, over 2,700 new teachers were hired, and 62 percent had no teaching credential. A report stated there were 5,400 teachers working with emergency credentials, more than double the amount prior to class size reduction. While the reform sounded good, the effect had a very deleterious effect in many districts. Inadequate teaching skills along with difficult-to-teach students have become an extremely serious problems in our schools. Unless this major educational deficit is corrected, our schools will fail even faster.

Time in School: Some educators would advocate adding 40 more days to the school year, which would increase its length by 22%. Americans could also lengthen the school day from 6 to 8 hours, which would mean a 33% increase in the time children spend in school each day. The arguments against this are the alternatives are too expensive, and there is no evidence it would substantially improve student achievement. Asian children who have longer school days have compiled an outstanding record of academic and professional achievement.

President Clinton, our "educational" president, suggested we lengthen our school year. The only major industrial country with a shorter school year than we have is Belgium. Every other nation with an advanced economy has a longer school year. The President was promoting national standards and testing programs as strategies to raise the standards of local schools. Opponents of these programs bring up the cost to financially poor school districts that would be forced to pay the additional expenses including higher teacher salaries, operating expenses, and costs for a longer school year.

Inept Teachers: The teacher in the room next to my "closet" where I tested the kids, regularly played a movie very loudly. When I went in to ask her about toning down the sound, the kids started yelling at me, "Hey! What's your name?" Not one or two kids, but half the class. The room was chaos, and the teacher told them to "Be quiet!" but there was no change in the noise level. She had absolutely no control over the class, and she played the movies every day loudly so the outsiders wouldn't hear the children's noise. She was a regular with years of experience, and everyone in the school knew about her problem. When I asked why wasn't anything done to either help her control the class or fire her, all I got in reply was a shrug. She wasn't removed because the principal knew it would take more trouble to get rid of her and to replace her than retain her. So who suffered? The kids, of course.

In order to terminate a teacher, the principal must take copious notes on the inappropriate teaching techniques, offer specific improvement remedies, and then observe, not only the inappropriate behaviors, but the addition or lack of use of the new methods. It takes considerable time, effort and energy that most principals do not have or care to give. The result is an incompetent teacher who is incapable, just playing the game and depriving children of a good education.

A teacher in Florida was outright incompetent. She did not prepare lesson plans, teach anything new for weeks at a time or get along with the students, and she couldn't be fired even though everyone was aware her performance was totally unsatisfactory. She underwent the usual procedure for getting rid of a teacher, an "improvement plan" the teacher must follow, but this one failed. She appealed her dismissal, and when that failed, appealed on up the court ladder with a union provided lawyer. Pete Wilson of California and George Voinovich of Ohio, both Republicans, fought for legal changes to allow the firing of inept teachers. The battle with their legislatures failed because the teachers' unions and allies resisted any major reforms. The bad teachers stayed on.

A bill introduced in the Florida legislature to fire incompetent teachers left untouched the tangle of dismissal procedures that made firing a bad teacher so complex and costly, (the average cost in Florida was $60,000) that few school districts even tried. The new bill, however, reduces from two years to 90 days the time teachers have to improve their performance before they can be fired. There may be hope for students, but the number of schools throughout the US where inept teachers continue forever is overwhelming. But if these teachers are fired—how will we replace them with qualified personnel? Students who have just one bad teacher have lower test scores than do comparable students with solid teachers. Bad teachers demoralize good teachers. It causes significant resentment among teachers who are working hard, and shows those who aren't that there is no consequence to low performance.

The NEA has received a great deal of pressure from politicians and parents alike because of their primary concern with teachers' wages and not defending teachers' jobs. At a representative assembly in the summer of 1997 over 9,000 NEA delegates voted to make some changes including more cooperation with school boards and administration in exchange for a bigger role in decision making. This would include more involvement in evaluating the quality of teachers by allowing teachers to rate their peers and take part in their dismissal. The rebuttal is that the system would pit teacher against teacher. Others objected because they felt it would put the union in the wrong position.

Under peer review and assistance, all beginning teachers as well as long-term teachers who were having teaching difficulties would be assigned a teacher or coach to help them improve. If they still didn't do a good job, they would be "encouraged" to leave. If that didn't work, a peer review panel would recommend dismissal. But would teachers have the right to protest the dismissal? The answer is probably, yes. Seattle and some schools in Ohio already had similar programs aimed at having experienced teachers help new teachers. Ineffective teachers are still a major problem.

Good Teachers: Tennessee's Project STAR (Student-Teacher Achievement Ratio) determined that the classes showing the most gains in reading and mathematics had the following characteristics:

- High learning expectations for all students. (This is the positive reinforcement that goes with the feeling students get from the teacher that they can learn and will learn. Many teachers are far more concerned with discipline than positive reinforcement.)
- Clear, focused instruction with enthusiasm. (New teachers have a difficult time with this approach since the teacher's presentation is often not "clear and focused," and there is generally little, if any, enthusiasm.)
- Carefully monitored student learning and progress. (Where is each student in the learning process?)

- Alternate methods of instruction when students did not learn. (A major mistake in US schools is that information/lessons are presented in one style, and if all the students do not master the learning, it is considered the students' fault, not the single-format lesson presentation.)
- Incentives and rewards to motivate students to learn, and praise for their success. (Positive reinforcement—a necessity in learning.)
- Efficiently managed classroom routines.
- High standards for classroom behaviors. (But not Cell Block tyranny.)
- A genuine "love" for children coupled with a sense of humor. The two basics of good teaching often ignored. The "love for the children" expressed by respect for them as individuals and appreciation for their efforts and skills; a "sense of humor" has a far more positive effect on class control than coercion.

The students in Project STAR out-performed students in larger classes in all grades (K-4) in reading, mathematics and basic study skills. The Parent-School Advisory Committee might look into assessing the quality of teaching in their child's school using the Project STAR teaching criteria to evaluate what is happening in the classroom.

Good teaching

A middle school teacher in one of the toughest districts in San Diego City Schools taught a class that included some youths who were difficult to handle in other classes. But in hers, they were very respectful. This gray-haired, small woman, called her students "Ladies" and "Gentlemen," in a quiet voice, and never yelled "shut up," or "be quiet!" The year began with consistent expectations of good behaviors from the students. Her lessons were well prepared, and she was always ready. She incorporated proper behavior expectations with kindness and consideration in her lessons. When a child misbehaved she took the student aside to discuss the problem in a quiet manner looking for a solution to the problem rather than scolding, punishment or humiliation. Her belief was that respectful ways of dealing with children is the basic reason for their good behavior. She has been a teacher for over 30 years. Good teaching is possible, but it takes understanding.

Teacher Inspiration: Motivation of the student by the teacher isn't easy, but here is one example of students being motivated beyond their wildest dreams. Barbara Vogel, a fifth grade teacher in Aurora, Colorado, read an article about modern day slavery in Sudan and Mauritania to her class which impressed them immensely. Some of the boys and girls burst into tears listening to the pain and suffering the slaves endured. Several students asked, "What can we do about it?" As one official said, "The children couldn't believe that slavery could exist in their time."

Students wrote letters and lobbied to end modern day slavery. When the word got out in the community, people chipped in and soon the amount to free the slaves grew to over $35,000. Next the students bought the freedom of many slave-people at about $50 per person. They organized STOP (Stop Slavery That Oppresses People) and channeled money through Zurich that went to middle men who bought the slaves and returned them to their homes. The students checked out the geographic areas of slave countries, wrote letters to politicians, and raised money—all initiated by the students' and the teacher's desire to help. The students served as excellent models for others. There is little doubt that many of the students' lives were changed by this idea and effort stimulated by an insightful teacher. While this response from students can't be assured every week in every class, imaginative teachers can produce this effect at times.

The US Department of Education is promoting a new program, the Mars Millennium Project, "An exciting youth initiative that challenges students across the nation to imagine and plan a community on the planet Mars for the year 2030 . . . One of the most exciting and engaging methods for teaching students mathematics and science in today's classrooms is the study of space and space travel. This field can also enrich arts and humanities lessons. Students can take virtual space voyages, chat on-line with space experts and researchers, design spacecraft, or with the help of architects, artists and engineers, devise plans for colonies on distant planets." A series of "Satellite Town Meetings" were arranged in partnership with a number of committees and business groups to promote the program. For more information, call 1-800-USA-Learn, visit http://www.ed.gov/inits/stm, or e-mail Satellite_town-Meeting @ed.gov.

The Department of Education also launched a Community Technology Center grant program for the start-up of centers that provide access to computers and related learning services for residents of disadvantaged urban and rural communities. For more information visit http//www.ed.gov/offices/OVAE/CT.

Curriculum Changes

> Learning is facilitated when the student participates responsibly in the learning process. When he chooses his own directions, helps to discover his own learning resources, formulates his own problems, decides his own course of action, lives with the consequences of each of these choices, then significant learning is maximized. There is evidence from industry as well as from the field of education that such participative learning is far more effective than passive learning.
>
> Carl Rogers, *Freedom to Learn* 1969

A basic part of Japanese education is building character in students, or *kokoro*, building mind and spirit. This involves the completion of the character of each individual into mentally and physically sound Japanese citizens who promote truth and justice, respect values of individuals, honor working and responsibility, and have a positive attitude as members of a peaceful country and society. In Japan many schools teach discipline, manners and moral education. Students are divided into groups of five or six, and each group is responsible for specific duties such as cleaning the classroom, serving lunch, or editing the classroom newspaper.

In the US we hear constant complaints about the lack of discipline and the need for students to develop habits that will make them productive employees. Yet American schools seldom teach "values," except for "Don't chew gum!" or "Raise your hand before you speak!" or "That lipstick isn't acceptable in this school!" The school's reply is academics and citizenship are the school's job; manners and morals or character education are the parent's job. Many times the parents do not have these skills to teach to their children. All children should receive adequate educations; not just some. The schools must produce these topics for building the type of students who will learn the skills for social survival or the skills will not be learned in many cases.

The topics listed should be covered in every public school beginning at kindergarten with the frequency depending upon the child's interests. These suggested courses will not supply information for good scores on the SAT, but they will help children survive in a changing world, and develop an understanding of coping skills that will make life much more meaningful and enjoyable.

Personal Education Program (PEP) The purpose of a personal education program is to establish long-term goals for the student which may not even last until the week-end. The program would be built around the student's interests and could change frequently. The bottom line, however, is the program places the student's interests and goals as the top priority in learning. Each student from the earliest grade possible would design a long-term program. The emphasis should be on the parent and teacher helping the student make decisions. Still the bottom line is that the program is the *child's* decision even if his choice at age 16 is garbage man or teacher's baby sitter.

Along with the PEP program, the teacher's long term goals would be measurement of learning styles, self concept, learning strengths and weaknesses, and the student's main interests. These measurements would begin as soon as possible at the beginning of each year. The teacher and the student need to understand these important parts of the student's personality in order to be effective in teaching and the learning process. The counselor and school psychologist could help.

Emotional maturity. *Emotional Intelligence,* a book by Daniel Goleman, could help provide some of the necessary subject matter to help develop emotional intelligence in children from birth on, especially in those children who have never had the help from their parents to develop emotional understanding. Goleman believes that "Our schools and our culture fixate on academic abilities, ignoring emotional intelligence, a set of traits. . . . (E)motional aptitude is a meta-ability, determining how well we can use whatever other skills we have, including raw intellect." This is the main point in the need for teaching these emotional skills— without them, other skills such as intelligence and enterprise are useless. The remedy he said, "must lie in *how we prepare our children for life.*" The major side effects of a lack of emotional intelligence lead to depression, eating disorders, unwanted pregnancy, aggressiveness and criminal behavior. Emotional skills are very important. It is an area in skill development that is often missing in children.

Social Sense. Teaching the children from K on about social behaviors, what is appropriate and what isn't; what is expected in a variety of situations, and what is not, and how to get along in our society is the major goal. This involves peers, practice, and video counseling from recordings of student behaviors, and talking about them with the student. "What happened? What were the alternatives? Was that your best choice?" More and more school-age children have no idea of what constitutes socially acceptable behavior. Class discussions of rules and regulations, what behaviors are appropriate, and which ones are not, could be a major topic. Group sessions with peers have also been effective. This area of learning socially accepted behaviors often can be very important to many children from the lower income areas to help them survive in school and be accepted by their peers. It could be an important part of every school curriculum.

How to control violence, anger, and resentment: Violence in schools has proliferated dramatically, frightening children and parents away from attendance. Conflict Resolution is a course that could be presented, emphasizing the fact that violence can be controlled and cured. There are a variety of programs dealing with this subject involving group meetings. Most have been successful, but children must be introduced to these programs to learn how to deal with anger and revenge. Some schools at present have officers to search students who are suspected of entering school with "weapons." The school needs more positive reinforcement for many parents who equate abnormal behaviors by a few students as characteristic of the entire school.

Sexual maturity. Schools should be teaching comprehensive sexuality courses, but are blocked in by those who feel that teaching about sex promotes sexual activity rather than prevention. Studies show that the opposite is true, and teenagers have declared that accurate information reduces sexual activities. Jane Pauley of TV's PBS cited studies that can reverse the disturbing trends, i.e., school sex education programs which balance a message of abstinence and the importance of birth control, along with community family planning clinics where teens are treated with respect. We need to build more of these programs immediately. The primary consideration involves the children born of these teenagers, and the lives they both will lead, the infant and the mother.

While AIDS is always a problem, there is also another danger to add to the risks of potential pregnancy and venereal disease — herpes type 2, for which there is no cure or vaccination. This is another disease that affects the infant prior to birth, and multiplies the problems in daily life. Herpes kills babies and can cause permanent and severe neurological damage for those who live. This increase in genital herpes, or herpes simplex virus type 2, is dangerous according to a report by the Centers for Disease Control and Prevention. Over 25.6 percent of women and 17.8 percent of men are chronically infected, according to the CDCP. This is 30 percent higher than in the 1976-1980 surveys. "There is no cure and no vaccine" according to the National Health and Nutrition Examination Surveys conducted by researchers at the federal Center for Disease Control and Prevention. Children must be made aware of these problems before they have sex, be informed of the possible consequences, understand how having unprotected sex can be damaging, and be aware of the ways to protect against infection. This is an important issue still unknown to a vast majority of children.

The Danger of Drugs. While there have been programs such as Nancy Reagan's, "Just Say No," DATE and DARE, their success ratios have been limited. Children need to be informed about what happens to many users who overdose and ruin their lives. I have worked with reforming drug users, and they were always willing to talk to other potential addicts about the dangers of drugs. Try to get known users to visit and take part in AA or drug rehab units, and listen to statements from peers about what drugs have done. There are drug prevention programs that work. Drug addiction today is now being classified by medical people as a biological problem rather than pure choice.

Raising Children. As it is now, raising a child for many parents, especially the pregnant teens, is primarily OJT. Parents must understand how to encourage verbal exchanges via coddling, talking, and stimulation; they need to know the various stages of brain development in children, and when the different types of stimulation are more successful. They need to know when the child is encouraging further stimulation and when the child is signaling enough. They need to learn how to control anger over an infant's behavior, and not abuse the child by shaking him or using other reactionary means that cause brain and other physical damage. This knowledge is extremely important in providing increased mental development so necessary in the early years of the child's growth.

Making Marriage Meaningful. This information would point out the benefits of legal marriage, what techniques could be used to keep a marriage a stimulating and lasting resource for both mates; how to make a commitment, what to look for in a mate, the influence of two parents on their children, and how to lessen the chances of divorce. Students need to understand why a marriage vow is part of a long-term commitment that has a tremendous influence on the life an infant will lead. There are a wide variety of resources to expand this concept. Our marriage rate has become a less important issue in spite of the problems children face in the one-parent family. Today marriage is growing as a less important practice among the 18 to 30 age group. Meeting couples who are living together, but are not married, is no longer unusual. The affect on children of the family breakup often has serious consequences. The affect from the break-up of parent relationships is devastating to nearly every offspring.

Finding Employment. Many business people would be more than willing to talk to classes about what is desired in an employable person, and what is not; what talents are needed, what jobs are available, and other employment information. If presented correctly, students could work on employment goals of their own. Children in the lower grades could begin to think about spending money on the needs that occur, and work up to how money is earned, as well as what is required to get a job.

Saving money and investing. A new coalition of financial and government organizations has put together various groups to help school children become financially literate. The Federal Reserve Board and the US Office of Consumer Affairs plus the American Financial Services Association, the Consumer Bankers Association, and the National Council on Economic-Education arranged uniform guidelines, standards and resources for teaching personal finance to students from kindergarten through the 12th grade. The Jump$tart Coalition for Personal Financial Literacy aims to have all high school seniors understanding how to handle their personal finances wisely by 2007. Volunteers from the investment field would be willing to talk about saving money to first graders and about mutual fund investment to high schoolers. Personal-Finance courses were offered to 60 percent of the high school students at West Middle Island School on New York's Long Island. It appears the children developed a healthy respect for spending and income. Schools can help children become financially aware of how to save and spend wisely.

Physical Education A study financed by the Chrysler Corporation Fund and administered by the Amateur Athletic Union found that children over eleven have become heavier and fatter. The number of students who can complete the components of a fitness test—strength, flexibility and muscular and cardiovascular endurance—has declined from 43 percent to 32 percent. While schools are promoting team sports, they are cutting back on physical education programs with only 36 percent of students in grades 5 through 12 taking daily physical education classes, and most grade-school children only once or twice a week. Only 15 percent of 12th grade boys and just 11 percent of senior girls take PE according to the US Surgeon General's office.

A study of about 4,000 children found that the obese children spend about four hours per day watching TV. Many urban parents discourage their kids from playing outside because of crime in the streets, so they spend their afternoons and evenings in the house. PE classes should emphasize fitness with muscle strength, muscle endurance, flexibility, body composition (what percentage of fat) and cardio-respiratory endurance. This appears equally as important in childhood health as any other subject in school. This could also help reduce students cigarette and alcohol consumption. Isn't it interesting that in our learning institutions, PE most often is "throw 'em a ball" instead of the stimulation of preserving and improving a healthy life style.

All of these subjects would be taught in an informal manner, the length of time depending upon the interest of the students, and the course altered to meet the needs of the particular group. The student's interests should be the major component of the program(s). The main resistance to these very needed subjects will come from those who believe our schools should produce students who excel in algebra, history, and science. Others will insist that higher standards be set for graduation, as if that would help any struggling student. They will also complain there isn't time in the present curriculum to teach these courses. These subjects would meet the direct needs of the students and the community. Algebra, on the other hand, wouldn't.

Problem Children: In every school there will be some few pupils who find it impossible to behave in class; they talk out of turn, fight with other students at recess, and generally cause chaos in the classroom. Each school should have a temporary area where these children can receive one-on-one help from a resource specialist, the counselor, the school psychologist, or anyone able to bring about changes in the child's behavior by teaching them the techniques of self control, curbing violence, interpreting antisocial events, and normal behavior. The main goal is to return these students to the classroom as soon as possible. Everyone should understand the removal is temporary. Student mediators could help; trained resource people could volunteer, and nowhere would there be a label, stigma or long term isolation from the regular class.

The counselor and school psychologist, if they have experience in group counseling, could take groups of students in sessions to talk about behaviors that are irritating, how to handle the situations, and areas that students would like help in controlling. This could also be done by teachers, but with the understanding, that with older students situations could arise that would require a great deal of tact and social skills. These group situations are very effective in some circumstances when students hear for the first time how others feel about certain actions, and the proposed remedies. Each class could also be instructed in how to deal with misbehaviors that disrupt and decide on how to deal with the problem.

The Internet: A factor that is rapidly changing learning, one that has features that will dominate information and lead to yet uncharted areas, is the growing internet, or "online school frontiers." The internet is expanding by leaps and bounds, is available day or night for young or old, and is expected to attract greater numbers of learners when on-line delays disappear with the advent of cable modems and the Internet 2 network now being built by US universities. At that point, students will be able to see and talk with one another in virtual classrooms.

Government aid is rapidly becoming available for more programs. California State University is opening a TeacherNet to provide a learning program for those teachers (about 30,000) who lack credentials to finish in half the usual time. While there are all kinds of fake programs and scams, there are moves for monitoring such programs by both state and federal governments. Check out the site of Council on Higher Education, http://www.chea.org to see if these programs have been accredited by the Department of Education. Since the internet has everything from sex to soybeans, every child should have access to the internet under the guidance of an adult for help and direction. E-mail alone will attract many students. For example, in one school I visited, students were contacting other students in Iceland and exchanging information. How many students even know where Iceland is located? In addition, with a simple PIN (number) in some schools a parent can call a school's web site to get current information on how the child is doing in grades, attendance, teacher comments, and other pertinent information. This interaction also lets the school know the child has an interested parent.

According to the US Department of Education as of March 1999, 51 percent of instructional rooms—classroom, computer or other labs, school libraries, and media centers—had internet access in 1998 compared to 27 percent in 1997 and three percent in 1994. The percentage of schools with internet access increased to 89 percent in 1998 up from 78 percent in 1997.

Some Innovations

> Children have a style of learning that fits their condition, and which they use naturally and will until we train them out of it. We like to say we send children to school to teach them to think. What we do, all too often, is to teach them to think badly, to give up a natural and powerful way of thinking in favor of a method that does not work well for them and that we rarely use ourselves.
>
> John Holt, *How Children Learn*, 1967.

Charter Schools: The Charter School program began in Minnesota in 1991 involving teachers in eight schools and spread quickly to six other states including California. Up to 100 schools were allowed to apply for charters in California authorizing them to operate free of the state rules and regulations such as the Education Code or reporting to a school board and the district bureaucracy. In turn charter schools were required to be reviewed every five years, meet standards for student achievement, and produce results that could be measured. The governor of California, Pete Wilson, recommended entire districts fall under the Charter School guidelines with enrollment in charter schools reaching more than 55,000 students.

This innovation in schools can change community education for the better, but it also has the potential for nepotism, corruption, and an even worse educational system. Organized as to style and content by groups of parents, teachers or outsiders to meet certain commu-

145

nity educational needs, Charter Schools are part of the public school system and are financed in the same manner as public schools. While they can choose their own courses of instruction, they must accept any student, and they are accountable to the local school boards for results. Accountability is based on a signed contract, and if the school fails to reach these goals, it can be shut down. Charter Schools may welcome dropouts, expelled students or students with learning problems. Their common goal, however, is to raise achievement standards.

One school district in California wanted to include an intensive program for first-graders who showed signs of falling behind in reading and math, after-school programs for gifted students, and, my favorite, a system for including severely handicapped students in regular classroom activities. This school was also working on contracts with parents so they could agree to spend so many hours on a variety of activities involving participating in the classroom, working with fund raisers, and making bulletin board items and designs at home. Parents who did not like a particular school system could choose to have their children bused to another school at the district's expense. Anyone can start a charter school, except for a private school already in operation. To open a charter school, detailed proposals must be submitted for approval, and once this is granted, the charter must be approved by the state board. Be sure to check out any changes in Charter school regulations in your city and state.

Santiago Middle School in Orange County, California, was funded by tax dollars, but was free from school district regulations. The student-teacher ratio was lower than other schools, but even more important, parents had to put in 12 or more hours per year as volunteers in anything that went on in the school from student trips, reading mentors, to cooking in the cafeteria or planting trees. The students wore uniforms, and graduation requirements became tougher — all without approval from Sacramento or a school board. With the endorsement of President Clinton, who called for greater parental choice in education and more publicly funded charter schools that operate outside the reach of teacher unions and the school-system bureaucracies, the charter school function is expected to grow.

The disadvantage with Charter schools was exemplified by a public school in a black district in Michigan. After years of declining enrollments, very low test scores, the problems parents found in management and money resulted in a decline in students. As the complaints about the school, grew the enrollment decreased from 5,000 in 1965 to about 1,750. In Arizona, the state with the most charter schools, enrollment is presently close to five percent of all students. Overall, the change may be for the better since unsuccessful schools appear the most likely to lose their student population—and why not?

Vouchers: When the voucher idea first was presented some time ago, many of us were enthusiastic about the possibilities of this innovation. The first thought was that it would create competition for public education and provide an escape for parents and their children from the incompetent schools. Much has changed since then. With parents sending their children to non-public schools via vouchers, the ADA declines, and this serves as the basis of the public schools' income. There is also a fear that only the parents from the upper SES groups will send their children off to private schools, leaving the student populations in urban and in lower income areas with harder-to-teach students. Families in the lower income areas will not be able to afford transporting their children across town, or the cost of tuition not covered by the voucher.

There are also several organizations that are fighting the Religious Right or the Christian Coalition over the voucher. The concern involves religious groups that will use private, religious schools as recipients of the vouchers and make religion, creationism over evolution and other religious beliefs, a part of the regular curriculum. In 1996, according to one source, the Christian Coalition spent $5.6 million in political donations. The Republican party also supported the voucher. It would appear to those who want religion taught in public schools that they must accept the teaching of a variety of religions, not just the espousal of one.

Education Secretary, Richard W. Riley, called taxpayer funded vouchers for private education a "fad" that would benefit a few students but not the majority. A "White Paper" put out by the Education Department warned that because of the limited number of private schools available to all students, only a small portion of the nation's 46.5 million public-school students would get the opportunity to attend private schools. In addition, most of the disadvantaged students would be left in schools drained of public funds, motivated parents and high achieving students. The paper added, "Instead of giving a few students a way out, we need to give all students a way up by improving the quality of all schools." Theodore J. Frostmann said, "If you are not a rich person, you are at the complete mercy of the education monopoly." Frostmann and John T. Walton, the heir to the Wal-Mart store fortune, set up a $200 million fund to help low-income families in Los Angeles, Chicago and other cities pay tuition for their children.

Many low-income parents would be unable to provide transportation for the their children to private schools. On the other hand, the evidence is that the more-educated, higher income, two-parent households do participate, leaving the poorest students behind in a declining school. An ACLU newsletter indicated that since the money for these vouchers would come from existing public school budgets, the poor children unable to use them will be stuck in public schools with declining budgets. The ACLU protested that vouchers are a fraud perpetrated on precisely the poor children they are intended to help as well as an unconstitutional windfall for religious schools. This is due to the majority of private schools being sectarian parochial schools, and the parochial schools' tuition is generally much lower than that of non-religious schools. This diverts public school funds primarily to religious schools whose admitted purpose is to proselytize their faith.

The Future: Secretary of Education, Richard Riley, pointed out in 1997 that we now have 52,000,000 students 18 years of age and younger, or 18% of our population. There has been a 50% increase in school enrollment in the last five years and school facilities for dealing with this increasing population are sadly lacking. There are more teachers, larger class sizes with achievement the number one problem. We also have an increase in the number of non-qualified teachers as test scores go down. He also stated we have one-third of the teachers who are now teaching out of their field. The long-term projection for our school systems is very poor. Significant steps must be immediately taken to help correct and improve our school systems nationwide.

Establishing a committee of concerned parents with the goal of helping to improve the schools is the first step. There are a variety of examples to choose from and grants to help with financing the (PSAC) committee's goals. Curriculum changes will be difficult to sell. Overcoming the committee members' opposition to these changes will take skill and talent. Think of the long-term goal in helping children to survive who are now being hopelessly lost in the mass of indifference affecting many communities. This goal should keep most of the committee members involved.

Some Questions to Ask

1. What business groups are involved in your school? If the school utilizes business groups, where does the money go? Does your committee approve of their contribution to learning?
2. Does your school have an accountability report card? If no, why not?
3. What is the length of the school time—students' and teachers'?
4. How would you rate your school—positive and negative qualities?
5. What are the possibilities of producing school reforms?
6. How would students, parents and teachers rate the school, individual teachers, the curriculum?

14217-PIER

7. Does the school have sufficient computers and teachers who can access the internet on a per-pupil basis?

8. What are the possibilities for curriculum changes?

9. Are the voucher or charter schools a problem for your school attendance?

10. How is the curriculum meeting the needs of the students and teachers?

11. What is the level of violence?

12. What changes have been made in the curriculum recently, if any?

13. What are the SAT, CBEST and other test scores for the school?

14. How is the violence in the school and neighborhoods rated?

15. Any classes that teach saving, paying debts, learning about spending?

PART FIVE

How Parents Can Rescue Our Schools

The real test then of a people's education is not so much the way they work or fight, but the way they use their leisure. To show excellent qualities in action and war, but in times of peace and leisure to be no better than slaves is to miss the happiness that is the end of human living.

Aristotle, *Man in the Universe*

Education is the number one issue in America, and what will be done is in the local area, not in Washington.

PBS, June 18, 1998.

Part Five explains how parents can check out their school for positive and negative qualities, financing school reforms, and suggests how to organize a Parent-School Advisory Committee (PSAC) to make changes. The power of parents for positive influence on schools is examined along with financing and school reform possibilities.

Checking Out the School

The future which we hold in trust for our own children will be shaped by our fairness to other people's children.

Marian Wright Edelman

School Accountability: In California, Proposition 98 requires all schools to provide information about their operation to the public via a school Accountability Report Card (ARC). Parents are also invited via the "Report Card" to attend meetings and ask questions. If your school doesn't have something like this, it could be the first step. One school ARC contained the following:

• A Student Profile: ethnicity graph, number of students, the mission and the goals of the school.

• Student Learning: Abbreviated Stanford Achievement Test (ASAT) scores in reading, math and language comparisons, student achievement, school to career transition, attendance, discipline, the climate for learning, and dropouts.

• Teaching Quality: A. assignments and teacher evaluation, B. substitutes, programs, instructional time, C. training and curriculum improvement, D. counseling and support service, E. textbooks and instructional material, F. class size, G. school facilities and safety, H. race and human relations.

• Shared decision-making, parent involvement, PTA, and community involvement.

• Finances: a budget, regular education, special education, sharing—teacher and administration.

This is a major part of the information every PSAC should obtain to help understand the school and determine necessary remedies.

While Proposition 98 in California required each school or district to provide a compendium of the school's test scores, attendance rates, teacher's salaries, dropouts, class sizes, and other data including 16 different items showing the school's performance, some schools did not follow this procedure. One district put out a single common Accountability Report Card for eight different schools. The largest district, on the other hand, published a six page, slick report, and put it online for computer users. One district failed to give the test scores as required, while another district published only the test scores for the high school results. Nine districts hadn't turned in ARC's for the previous year. Proposition 98 also asked for a report on the school's progress in meeting its goals in reading, writing, and arithmetic plus "other academic goals." Some schools avoided this, as well.

One ARC had six pages that started with the past school accomplishments and awards, followed with graphs of the schools' ethnic populations, test scores from 1994 on up including the California Learning Assessment System (CLAS), and the California Test of Basic Skills (CBEST) over the past three years, attendance over the past four years, and enrollments over the past seven years. Parents need to put more pressure on the administration to receive accurate ARC's, and to examine the report carefully.

While an ARC example may look good with important information, it can also contain information that is dated and inaccurate. One school's "Report Card" issued in 1996 used achievement data from the years 1992-93 to compare test scores to look as if they had recently improved. Other reports use eloquent language in describing learning programs that would require angels to do the teaching. These newsletters can, however, provide a base from which to start and to ask questions.

Meeting the School Personnel

Meeting the people who can strongly influence your children's future is very important. Present yourself as a concerned parent or a member of the committee who wants to help the children get the most out of school—one who wants to help the principal do the best he or she can. Educators are defensive. Be a friend.

The Principal: Principals do a tight rope, balancing act between the district office, ordering supplies, and dodging angry teachers. Good administrators can make a bad teacher better by helping to improve the teacher's instructional techniques and skills. Unfortunately what some principals do is make good teachers worse by treating them as inferiors who must become obsequious to ensure a favorable evaluation, and who must play games with students because there is little to no support from the administration.

The principal is extremely important in establishing school reform. The teachers may all be enthused about your school-based management system (PSAC) that includes both you and them, but without the principal's overt support, the program could die a natural death. Natural, because the principal in many cases can squeeze the teacher with duties and details, that drain any teacher-parent management system until it's dry. Many principals, when talking with parents, will slip into the PR mode to tell you how little money there is available, how enrollments are increasing as the budget is decreasing, and the multitude of problems involved in the school operation.

SOME QUESTIONS TO ASK: The following questions may be threatening to some principals, so try to place them in the framework of helping the principal improve the school. It will also be assumed that you haven't read the school handbook in advance. Make sure you have.

• What is the size of the teaching staff and the turnover each year? What is the teacher-pupil ratio?

The turnover is important because it may be an indicator of teacher dissatisfaction with the school. The turnover may have been zero the previous year because all the good teachers had already left, but it may give you an introduction to principal-staff relationships. The pupil-teacher ratio will probably be too large, and the principal will talk about how short the school is on money available to hire more teachers.

• How many teachers are licensed or certified, non-qualified, or hired as temporary? Is there is a shortage of teachers in your area?

Non-qualified persons are often hired under various conditions to permit them to teach for a year or more. To improve your school, insist on only qualified teachers and help to find them. This will be difficult due to the shortage of qualified personnel.

155

• Are there enough substitute teachers?

In Los Angeles, for example, there may be about 1,200 teachers absent each day, and there aren't enough substitutes available. Sometimes the solution is to shuffle children from one class to another, often at levels far below or far above where the children are currently functioning. This is not education and not even good baby sitting. If there aren't enough subs, what happens to the child when the teacher is absent? Very often, the lesson plans for an absent teacher are aimed at keeping the class busy and the substitute safe.

• How many teaching days are missed due to teacher training programs and other "necessities?" California had eight days with teachers absent in "training seminars." What happens to the students when the teacher is absent?

• What major problems does the school face such as drugs, truancy, dropouts, fighting and violence? How are these various problems handled? What's the percentage of transient students?

Does the principal know the severity of the school's transients: These are the students who come and go and will increase a class size to 35, and then drop it to 20. Learning takes continuity, and yet some schools have a transient population per year approaching 50 percent. This change over in student population brings down the level of learning. Watch out for a speech of generalizations lacking specifics.

• How many activities does the school have each year such as assemblies or field trips that interrupt class time? Are they worthwhile?

Many schools regularly let students out of class for these "worthwhile activities"; the local band, pep rallies, some visiting speaker, a cause, a field trip to a bakery, etc. A few of these may be worth the time out of class, but many are not.

• How does the school handle behavior problems — expulsion, suspension, zero tolerance, detention?

This will tell a great deal about the school and the range of problems—more particularly it will tell about the school's attitude toward punishment. The rate of suspensions and how they are handled will also reveal whether the school is punishment oriented or more prone to helping students.

- How recent are the text books? What is the date of publication, age and grade level—the interest level? How often renewed? Look at the textbooks, not only the ones your child uses, but have your committee check out as many as possible. Do they meet the children's needs? Are they "dumbed down?" Do they miss or evade the important elements your committee deems a priority? Do they deal with subjects, or are they selling pap as opposed to particulars? Are the first two chapters more devoted to last year's learning for those who have forgotten over the summer or failed to learn what was necessary? Is this a waste of time and space in a "new" textbook? How current are they?

This may be a more appropriate question for an individual teacher, but it will allow the principal to vent on the inability to get money out of the district for textbooks. Are there enough textbooks for each child? How is the school fixed for supplies? Do teachers have enough paper, etc.?

- Is the school accredited?

There should be an accrediting agency of some form from a group such as the North Central Accreditation Association (NCAA). The accreditation doesn't really mean much; something like the Good Housekeeping Seal of Approval. If your school hasn't passed or is marginal, what is the reason?

- What is the purpose of school—of education?

Make sure you have plenty of time for this one because the principal may get out the soap box. You'll hear such things as: transmitting our cultural heritage, (often emphasized in multi-cultural schools), developing productive and useful citizens, a preparation for life, an ability to assume a responsible place in our society, democracy, employment, citizenship, etc. If the principal says, "To help children become life-time learners," you've got a winner. Try this same question on the teacher(s). Before you leave, drop the name of the superintendent.

The committee needs to know about violence in the school. How is it handled? Is suspension the main behavior changer (one that doesn't work) for offenses ranging from drugs to truancy? What about gangs? Do minorities get suspended more frequently and dispropor-tionately than Anglos? The answer to that is "yes" in nearly every school.

Also, many parents have little idea how much school time is spent in non-classroom activities between kindergarten and graduation. If a pep rally for a dart team takes precedence over a math class, for example, then somebody should point out the proper priorities to the principal. Ask about after-school activities. Doing all of this will help you learn a lot about the school and about education. You will gain a view of the school that is totally different from sitting at home, or in PTA meetings, or reading the Parent-School Bulletin. It will also help your committee reach positive conclusions.

The Teacher: Teachers are likely to be more defensive than principals. Try to assure the teacher that you are interested in working for the education of children. For insecure teachers, threatening statements could result in a negative attitude towards a child. Teachers are human, too, and have the same frailties. Like the rest of us, they find ways to get even for assumed slights. You want to work *with* the teacher to help children learn. It is important to convince the teacher of this.

Ask the teacher some of these questions in a way that allows the teacher to express feelings without repudiation.

• What are the teacher's views on class control and punishment?
   Is positive reinforcement or individual and class punishment em-

phasized? Is concern about class control and disciplines so strong that the teacher comes across as more of a warden than an educator? Are problems handled individually, or is there a single rule that fits all? Is the class emphasis on humiliation and punishment, or rewards and positive reinforcement? Is coercion the answer?

• Homework — How much and how often? Can it be done in class? What value does it have on the final grade? How will you know, as a parent, if your child has been assigned any homework?

For some teachers doing homework correlates with the Puritan concept of industriousness, and this omission will result in failing a class even if test scores are excellent. William Glasser in his book, *THE QUALITY SCHOOL*, advocated no homework since students will want to do the learning in class when their interests are aroused and follow-up on their own outside of class· How about the grading system?

How much of the final grade do daily, weekly, or quarterly grades count? How about projects? What is important on a paper: content, spelling, grammar, or originality? You may have heard about the paper graded by ten different teachers that received ten different scores since the value judgments of the teachers were based on different criteria ranging from spelling to ideation.

• How many children failed last year? The last few years?

If the teacher doesn't believe in failing children, it may be that the emphasis is on positive reinforcement. If five or six children failed out of 25 to 30, you should ask why. (Read the section on "Retention.")

• Where does the teacher plan to go with the class educationally?

If the reply is a cut-and-dried plan that says we're going from A to Z as the curriculum demands with no stops in between, this may mean trouble. Look for flexibility, adjustment to where the individual students are, adaptability as opposed to concern with content. Many teachers fear that if the children in their class do not do well on some school-wide tests, then the teachers will be rated lower by the principal. This use of children's test scores for evaluation of teachers is forbidden in many states, but still the fear prevails and often for good reason. Therefore, many teachers want to complete the curriculum at any cost to insure better scores on the standardized tests. Some teachers cheat to help their pupils score better on these tests as has been shown in several studies, which, of course, isn't learning. We need someone who is concerned with the child first and the curriculum second. Yes, it may be important to cover certain materials, but it is also important for the student to be realistically involved in that learning. If he or she isn't interested, then meaningful learning doesn't take place. Ask the teacher how he or she likes the job. Are there plans for long-term teaching, or leaving next year? There are many teachers who are just hanging on. They dislike the job and the kids, but have no alternatives except only eight years 'till retirement.

As a parent, another important benefit of meeting the child's teacher(s) is that your child will no longer be a face without a background. After your meeting, your child takes on an identity with a concerned parent who can help—who cares. When it comes time to grade a paper, a test, or a report, the fact that the teacher knows a parent is involved affects the grade—particularly if you come across as an assertive parent who will help, not a hostile one who is out for a pound of flesh. The same will hold true when your child needs to be disciplined in school—unless you have an angel.

If the teacher knows the parent and the child, grades can be boosted by the self-fulfillment prophecy. Rosenthal explained in his book, *PYGMALION IN THE CLASSROOM,* how the self fulfilling prophecy works. The experimenters took some children's names at random, some literally out of a hat, and told the teachers that these students were "late bloomers" and would soon begin to do well. Lo and behold, the children did improve. The experimenters found that the only factor that changed was the teacher's expectations of the students. The teacher thought the children would do well and they did. Want to try this on your child's teacher? (1)

The Counselor: Counselors are a different breed. Some go into the profession because they want to get out of the classroom at any cost; others to help children by "counseling" and pointing them in the right direction; still others as the path to become an administrator. They usually are easier to deal with than the principal or teacher, and often have a better idea of what is going on in the school in terms of what teacher is having trouble and which ones are doing well, and who are the "bad" students.

What are the major school problems: drugs, truancy, violence? The counselor should be in a better position than the principal to give you accurate information. Ask about the teachers to confirm the committee's research. The counselor is usually more informed since they often listen to student's complaints about this or that teacher. . . . seldom accolades.

Ask about the school-wide, standardized tests given to the student body. Who sees the results? Are parents and teachers allowed to review them or are they sent to the state bureaus and never heard of again? Is an item analysis done to show what the children are and are not learning? An item analysis is a computer search of how the children did on the test, usually by grades, with each question or group of questions defining areas where the children have learned the subject matter and where they are deficient. Are teachers shown the results? Are the results explained to all concerned?

The only reason for testing children is to find out where they are in the learning process and what they still need to be taught. If these standardized results are examined carefully via computer, the results will show what class, for example, did well in fractions, but poorly in carrying numbers in subtraction. These deficiencies can then be remedied. Unfortunately, this item analysis is seldom done in a meaningful manner for teachers or parents.

Ask about the school dropout rate? Nationwide the figure varies from 14% in some communities to 50% in some urban areas. How about college preparation courses in the school; college catalogues, college entrance exams (the SAT, ACT, PSAT, etc.), and what percentage of the student body is admitted to colleges after graduation? If it is a very low percentage that goes on to college or if the counselor doesn't know the answer, try to find out why. Ask how much time the counselor spends talking to children as opposed to shuffling paper. If you find one of your child's teachers not to your liking, start with the counselor and ask for a class change. Mention a "personality conflict" which seems to cover a multitude of sins. If the counselor ducks the issue, go to the principal; from there to the superintendent, and then to the board of education—or just change schools. You should also decide if the counselor is the kind of person you would like talking to your child on a very personal level.

The committee can also check out the financial status of their school(s) as was done by EdSource in California. The 16-page report is titled, "How California Compares." Some of the 1996-97 data that compared California with other states and the District of Columbia for 1996-97 indicated California was:

> First in the number of students
> Ninth in teacher salaries
> 37th in high school graduation rates
> 41st in per-pupil expenditures
> 47th in students per computer
> 50th in students per teacher and students per principal

While it may be time consuming and less than a thrill, get to know your school-board members; who they are, what their educational goals are and how they function on the board. Be aware at school board election time who is what, and if you want that person formatting school policy. Many people run for the school board as a springboard into the political arena. Once on the school board they'll do all kinds of stunts to appeal to groups that might help them along the political escalator. Check them out regularly to ensure they are school-goal oriented.

Some goals your PSAC might consider:

1. A competent teacher in every classroom which will create differences in what is meant by "competent."

Parent involvement whenever possible both at home and school.

2. Principals who will lead and take responsibility for both success and lack of learning.

3. Accountability for teachers and the principal based on where the child has progressed from the first entry into the school/class based on where the child was educationally.

4. A curriculum based on children's needs, not on passing tests.

5. A restriction on coercion in the school and an emphasis on positive reinforcement.

6. Reading based on the child's needs with an early beginning prior to school entry.

7. Introduction of subject matter based on the child's interest and needs.

8. Promotion of special help for low income families in early learning skills.

(See Appendix C for more information on early learning skills instruction.)

Organizing A Parent-School Advisory Committee

The well educating of their children is so much the duty and concern of parents, and the welfare and prosperity of the nation so much depends upon it, that I would have everyone lay it seriously to heart.

John Locke, 1692, in a letter to Edward Clarke

I know of no safe depository of the ultimate powers of the

14217-PIER

society but the people themselves; and if we think them not enlightened enough to exercise their control with a wholesome discretion, the remedy is not to take it from them but to inform their discretion.

Thomas Jefferson

The most profound education begins in the home.

Ronald Reagan, Republican Convention, 1992.

Give your community and its children a valuable gift—your time and talents. By supporting your schools through the gift of yourself and your resources, you strengthen your community, lead by example and send a strong message to children that their educational success is important.

President Bill Clinton, *America Goes Back to School.*

If the Ford Motor Company continued to produce the Model T simply because it sold so well many decades ago, the company would not only go bankrupt, but be the subject of much ridicule as well. Yet, the public schools in a non-competitive environment, a state enforced monopoly, continue to adhere to an ancient model, and steadfastly refuse to change in spite of nationwide criticism and outright derision. Like the dinosaur, it is too large, it is not adapting to its environment, and it is dying.

The following organizations can help establish a PSAC with suggestions on operation procedures. Without reforms, our schools will continue to fail.

Parents for Public Schools: In 1991 PPS was incorporated as a national organization with a unique model for organizing parents. Today "Parents for Public Schools (PPS) is a national organization of grassroots chapters dedicated to recruiting families to public schools, involving parents in more meaningful roles (as decision makers), and improving public schools community wide through district level involvement. We believe that offering every child the highest quality of public education is vital to American democracy. By mobilizing parents who reflect our diverse culture, we build excellent public schools and better communities."

Here are some of their emphasized convictions:

- *An attitude of ownership.* Parents' rights and responsibilities help make schools the best they can be.
- *A conviction about community.* Parents are the bridge between schools and the communities they serve. The community relies on the public schools to train its citizens, and the schools require essential community support and affirmation to do the best job.
- *An understanding that a priority must be a priority.* Parents are rolling up their sleeves and tackling tough quality issues at the school district level.
- *A willingness to raise the bar.* Public schools need parents challenging notions of mediocrity and working to set and meet the highest possible standard.
- *A wider lens for viewing public school success.* Test scores are important, but student achievement can and should be measured by a mixture of variables. The community at large—especially the external, vocal critics—needs to know there is something to be said for the quality of schooling found in the arts, physical education and extracurricular opportunities. School should be fun, not just a production line for a future work force.
- *Professional skills.* PPS members are freely giving expertise they have fine-tuned at the workplace — critical thinking, data analysis, strategic planning, goal setting and resource development.
- *Recruiting and mentoring others.* Willing parents are paving the way for those who are less inclined to be on the front lines, helping them find their niche while continuing to fill their own.
- *Patience, but persistence.* The envelope PPS parents push may not be recognized as a benefit to schools—yet. Districts and building level personnel may not welcome or know what to do with parents. They may feel threatened or simply overwhelmed. As critical friends, PPS parents are teaching school districts how to tap their expertise and insight.

• *A sense of humor and optimism.* There is a high road to this work, although parents often feel stuck in the trenches. Membership is growing as parents realize constructive involvement can be enjoyable, worthwhile and fruitful. (From the Parents for Public Schools, "Parent Press," special issue).

PPS gave the following suggestions in their summer 1999 issue of *Parent Press* for "A Balanced Approach to Choice" when choosing a school:

· What are the choices or options currently available in the system for parents to participate in the improvement of public schools?
· Do parents have a fair and open chance to participate in the policy debate around school choice ideas?
· Will there be a governance or oversight role for parents in the proposed policy?
· Will the policy ensure open and fair admissions for all students?
· Will the policy result in a fair distribution of financial and human resources for all students?
· How will the district ensure that schools involved are accountable to the public?
· How will the district ensure that all innovations or positive learnings derived from this experiment help to improve the system as a whole?

For more information contact the PPS Clearinghouse at 800/880-1222 or refer to our website at parents4publicschools.com.

"Parents for Public Schools now has an organizational presence in 15 states." While individual chapter activities and goals vary, a wide variety of support, services, and technical assistance is available from the PPS national network which encompasses communities and education advocates across the country. The national office provides resources and technical assistance to local chapters, so that chapters start going, keep going and do great work along the way. As chapters are organizing, PPS national staff offer specific services including speakers for an introductory/

information meeting, connections to established chapter leadership in other communities, and technical assistance in developing a work plan. To request information and materials, address the national Office, 1520 N. State St. Jackson, MS 39202 (601) 354-1220, fax (601) 353-0002

According to Joyce Epstein of Johns Hopkins University, a researcher on parent involvement, "The strongest and most consistent predictors of parent involvement at school and at home are the specific school programs and teacher practices that engage and guide parent involvement." For a copy, write to: Center for Law and Education, 1875 Connecticut Avenue, NW, Suite 510, Washington, DC 20009. Phone (202) 986-3000, e-mail cledc @erols.com.

The US. Department of Education has a number of issues of "Community Update" that offers examples of school change. The July/August 1999 edition has "America Goes Back to School 1999-2000: Challenge Our Students and They Will Soar!" They point out that this program can help communities "rally around an area of interest such as: making schools safe and drug free; recruiting and preparing quality teachers; modernizing schools; expanding after-school summer programs; getting high standards into every classroom; or developing pathways to college and careers." Examples are given of schools that utilized these techniques and succeeded. For a free copy of the Organizers Kit or publications designed to help families, community members and business get involved in education, call 1-877-4ED-PUBS; or call 1-800 USA-LEARN or visit http://pfie.ed.gov.

Financing School Reform

Title I (Aid for Disadvantaged Children) consists of $7.23 billion of the overall $15.5 billion appropriated. Within Title I is Section 1118 which addresses parent involvement within a local education association (LEA). An LEA may receive funds under this part only if it implements programs, activities, and procedures for the involvement of parents. LEA's must "coordinate and integrate parental involvement strategies such as Head Start, Even Start, Early Start, Parents as Teachers (PAT) program, the Home Instruction Program for Preschool Youngsters (HIPPY), and state-run preschool programs." (See Part Six for more information on PAT and HIPPY.)

The purpose of Title I, as stated in the bill, is "to enable schools to provide opportunities for children served to acquire the knowledge and skills contained in the rigorous state content standards and to meet the challenging state performance standards developed for all children under the Goals 2000, Educate America Act, or in their absence under this title." The legislation goes on to list standards which include providing children with enhanced educational opportunities, school wide reform, professional development, coordinated services, and *"affording parents meaningful opportunities to participate in the education of their children at home and at school."* Title I can pay for some of the expenses the committee may incur helping families. Section 1118 of the Improving America's Schools Act of 1994 describes these efforts. For more information on Title I call 202-260-0965.

For the public sector, write to:

Catalog of Federal Domestic Assistance
Superintendent of Documents
US Government Printing Office
Washington, DC 20402

In California write to:

Orange County Center
1000 E. Santa Ana Blvd. Ste 200
Santa Ana, CA 92705
Call (714) 953-1655
For Los Angeles call (213) 413-4042

Transition Grants: Getting a grant to operate a PSAC sounds easy, but it isn't. There may be restrictions such as "no longer than 25 pages, double-spaced and written in 10-point type or larger." I have taken a seminar in grant application, but I still will find someone who has applied for a grant successfully and work with them. There is a language that works in the application, and plain English isn't it.

For further information, try "Developing Winning Grants," a governmental publication that provides "Grant Information Resources." The US Department of Education on its website reported, "The Student Guide 1999-2000 tells how to apply for grants, loans, and work-study, the three major forms of student financial aid available through the federal Student Financial Assistance Programs. This guide is the most comprehensive resource of student financial aid from the Department."

Involving Businesses: When it comes to improving schools, employers have numerous options: They can provide resources for one or more schools, they may donate used equipment or special expertise, and employees may be given time off to volunteer. General Mills in Georgia formed a partnership with a neighborhood elementary school. Employees gave plant tours, helped build playground equipment, and visited the school to give talks on subjects such as careers. But some good businesses will expect a return other than "thanks" for the contribution.

"Employers, Families, and Education," a booklet from the US Department of Education on "Building Community Partnerships for Learning," has valuable information on involving businesses in committee goals. Each chapter is headed by a statement from a business leader. For example, Robert E. Allen, Chief Executive Officer, AT&T pointed out, "We have not traditionally linked the well-being of children to the success of business or the governance of nations. Yet increasingly we're acknowledging that upheavals in the American family aren't self-contained; they intersect with business and economic circles and loop into the social fabric of this nation. As a society, we assume a larger affiliation—one that implies, not just family ties, but added obligations."

Some Business Programs: A grant from the Technology Literacy Challenge Fund, a $5 billion, five-year program to integrate technology into school classrooms, involves money intended to hire teachers, put computers and other software into classrooms, and wire schools into the Internet. Priority so far has gone to poor schools, schools with no internet connections, low computer-student ratios and few teachers with technology training. This would be worth the investigation.

Ambassadors for Education, a program developed by the National Association of Partnership in Education (NAPE), has a three-part, hands-on workshop designed to get community members more involved in the schools. Some employers such as Con Edison of New York City, People's Gas of Tampa, Florida, and UNUM Life Insurance have sponsored these work-shops for their employees.

• Parenting for Education, a seminar series developed by US West Education Foundation to promote school success, is utilized by employers and community groups which purchase the 8-hour program.

• Meld is a family support system that provides information for teen mothers and fathers, single parents, and parents of children with special needs.

• Some employers such as Merrill Lynch and HBO keep family resource libraries where employees can borrow books or videos.

• Ohio Bell has a teen line; a telephone hotline that provides counseling specifically on teen-related issues.

• *Parent Power* published by Ashland, Inc., the Family Education Network, is available on www.ashland.com/education.

• *Employers, Families and Education* gives examples of what employers can do to support family involvement in education. Call 1-800 USA LEARN to request a copy. Be sure to find out the goals the business ventures wish to achieve.

PART SIX

MAKING CHANGES

By education most have been misled.
So they believe because they were bred.
The priest continues what the nurse began, and thus the child imposes on the man.

John Dryden 1631-1700

There is, on the whole, nothing on earth intended for innocent people so horrible as school. To begin with, it is a prison. But is in some respects more cruel than a prison.

George Bernard Shaw 1856-1950

Don't try to teach a pig to sing.

It annoys the pig and wastes your time.

Anon

Students who enter school without the essential development in verbal, social and emotional skills are increasing in number. Part Six explains how Parent-School Advisory Committees can alleviate some of these deficiencies by showing the parents of at-risk children the functions necessary for normal development based on specific programs that have been proven effective. The concern is stimulation for brain growth in infants in the first years of life along with continued reinforcement, and helping "at-risk" children with the necessary programs that have been successful. Help for pregnant teens, curbing violence, drug usage and the dropout rate along with the promotion of democracy are also included. A description of Community Learning Centers is examined as another alternative or as an adjunct to public schools.

Programs to Increase Infant Learning

Parents as Teachers (PAT) a program based on research shows the first three years of life are essential learning years, and that parental involvement is an important contributor to the child's success in school. Burton White of Harvard University established New Parents as Teachers (NPAT) as a successful operation after much research. From 1981 to 1985 about 350 families in four Missouri school districts took part in the pilot phase of PAT. These districts included urban, suburban and rural communities with participating parents from all ages and groups. When children in the pilot project reached age three, a randomly selected group was tested against a carefully matched comparison group. Results of this evaluation, conducted by an independent research firm, confirmed the benefits of PAT. At age three, children in the pilot project were:

• Significantly more advanced than other children in language development.

• Significantly ahead in problem solving and other intellectual abilities.

• Significantly advanced in demonstrating coping skills and positive relationships with adults.

About 1,500 trained "parent educators" worked with over one hundred thousand Missouri families with children from birth to age five who participated in the statewide program. All parent educators were trained in child development and parent education. These educators visited the families, formed group meetings, and did annual developmental screening of language and motor development. Interested parents enrolled in the program, which provided continuous service from the third trimester of pregnancy until the child reached the age of three. The program provided:

- Monthly visits to the home by parent educators trained in child development.
- Monthly group discussion meetings with other parents.
- A parent resource center in a school offering learning materials for families and facilities for child care.

PAT parents were:

- More knowledgeable about child-rearing practices and child development, including the use of constructive discipline. This is vital information.
- Were more likely to rate their school districts as very responsive to their children's needs; the figure for PAT parents was 55% compared with 29% for control group parents. PAT parents and children performed well, regardless of socioeconomic disadvantages and other traditional risk factors.

A PAT book from the University of Missouri, St. Louis is a massive volume that covers everything from nutrition to toilet training. Instruction in PAT is provided by a professional staff from the New Parents as Teachers Model Project providing a 30 hour program of "intensive instruction on: Program Organization and Management, Marketing PAT in your Community, Conducting Home Visits & Group Meetings, Monitoring Children's Progress, Recruiting Families, Evaluation." See References for literature on PAT and a phone number.

For more information on this program write to Parents as Teachers: The National Center Marillac Hall, University of Missouri-St. Louis, 8001 Natural Bridge Road, St. Louis, MO 63121 (314) 553-5738. Or write Early Childhood Education Section, Department of Elementary & Secondary Education, PO Box 480, Jefferson City, MO 65102-0480 (314) 751-2095.

The Home Instruction Program for Preschool Youngsters (HIPPY) was developed in 1969 by the National Council of Jewish Women (NCJW) Research Institute for Innovation in Education at The Hebrew University of Jerusalem, Israel. Since then it has grown into a world-wide movement. First Lady Hillary Rodham Clinton in a letter to HIPPY, May 1993, wrote, "HIPPY is making a vital contribution to the education of young children. It teaches parents to prepare their children for school and promotes a unique partnership between educators, parents, and children. I commend you on your commitment to fostering a love of learning and strengthening the bonds between parents and children."

HIPPY chooses parent-instructors who are members of the community and in the parent program themselves. They visit other participating member's homes biweekly and instruct using the HIPPY educational materials. Evaluations of the program have shown success, plus interesting changes between the parents and children. First the relationship between the parents and their children begins to improve, then the parents' experience a boost of self confidence and a new perception of the important role they play in their children's lives.

The HIPPY program also found:

1. Parents felt empathy with the enormous task facing their children's teachers.
2. Parents wanted to know more about what was happening in school, specifically in their child's classroom.
3. School personnel began to take parents and their concerns more seriously.
4. Parents felt a growing sense of self-esteem. As the HIPPY Start-up Manual says on page 12: ". . . . (A)ll share a common belief that parents are the primary educators of their children, and all have a strong commitment to enhancing the role that parents play in supporting their children's learning and development."

"I have long admired the success of your HIPPY program in enabling parents to become their children's first teachers. I look forward to the day when HIPPY USA has brought the program to every community in the US." — President Bill Clinton in a letter dated March 18, 1993.

See Appendix C for more on HIPPY.

The Brookline Early Education Program (BEEP) promoted the idea that high quality, family oriented, comprehensive education during the first five years of the child's life could serve as a community base for primary education activities, ensuring that children enter kindergarten as healthy, competent learners. There were three major components — parent education and support, early childhood education for toddlers and pre-kindergartners, and health and development monitoring.

The results demonstrated that an intensive level of intervention during the first five years positively modifies subsequent classroom behavior and academic skills. This effect was most pronounced for children from less educated families. The children at greatest risk for school difficulties benefited from the program, "but only if the preschool services were intensive." Their findings in this five-year study involving children who received the services, found that public schools can launch and sustain large-scale, complicated pre-school reforms successfully, that parents from all backgrounds can be meaningfully involved in better preparing their children for public education, and that a multidisciplinary approach works in this process.

Their philosophy was parent oriented:

1. Parents are the most significant educational force in the life of the child; therefore, parents and staff need to become partners during all stages and in all components of an early education program. Both parents and staff members need to be involved in planning for the child's educational needs.

2. Family styles and cultural preferences should be respected. Specific methods were not prescribed for parental interaction, but rather the staff members found effective ways of interacting that were compatible with the parents' abilities and values. This is important.

3. Services made available to the parents were not pre-packaged, but

rather fitted to the individual family needs. For example, discipline was approached from the particular family's orientation rather than a fixed method.

Those who teach parents these skills should be particularly aware of #2 on the list above: "Family styles and cultural preferences should be respected. . . . Specific methods should not be prescribed," which means no one set program for all parents; instead, individualized differences. This will produce more cooperation.

The necessary practices included:
- The importance of the child in contributing to stimulation practice as opposed to being a passive recipient of teaching.
- Knowledge of the parent as to where the child is in ability and interests to ensure the stimulation is effective at the right time and place.
- Providing questions and stimulation that promote verbal problem solving to expand thinking as opposed to one-word answers such as. "What is the name of—?"
- Meeting the child's level of development with stimulation, questions, and toy levels.
- Taking advantage of the learning-teaching institutions in the neighborhood on a daily basis, whenever possible.
- Promoting reading, writing, art, sports, visits to libraries, and more.
- A regular reading program at a regular place with available tools such as desk, pencil, book(s), etc., and asking questions about the reading.
- Making use of stimulating toys.
- Utilizing a parental style that is "responsive, flexible, concerned with positive regard, and accepting of the child's ideas, suggestions and feelings."
Unfortunately, BEEP is no longer in operation.

The **Early Childhood Family Education** (ECFE) program for the Minnesota Department of Education was established in 1984 and operated in 365 school districts. Lois Engstrom, a program supervisor, described the family education: "We have found that setting up shop for our work wherever parents were meeting to receive food stamps for feeding programs helped a lot. The parents sort of stand off and watch, and aren't usually eager to ask for our help. We show them some hands-on activities, and eventually the parents become more interested and start asking questions about their children. They then are invited to join in parents groups."

She explained how parents in the program recommend ECFE to other parents. Her staff always works through the parents, and does not try to take over the responsibility of the child. The parents find this approach very different. Usually the social worker or the person handing out the food stamps suggested to the parents what to do, when to do it, and how often. "It turns them off just like it would us. I think we have a long way to go — but its coming! Early Childhood Education is without a doubt the most exciting and rewarding adventure in education that I have experienced" (Lois Engstrom, Program Supervisor, The Minnesota Early Childhood Family Education Program).

Available in the state's 350 school districts the "ECFE program teaches new parents everything from how to stimulate babies' brain growth with books and games to how to recognize signs of delayed development, or make toddlers behave. There are classes for dads, for families who speak only Spanish, for hearing impaired parents, and gay and lesbian families. There are programs for first-time parents, reading lessons for those want to start school and home visits for those who can't get away."

Providing parenting programs for new parents has rapidly become the thing to do in many states. In Elmira, N.Y., David Olds launched a program of home visits with new parents in 1978. The program of intensive home visits teaches new and expectant parents how to interpret and respond to their babies' cries, to recognize developmental delays, and how to play with children. The model Olds pioneered in upstate NY has been extended to 14 low-income communities. His parenting programs are designed to reduce malfunctioning brain growth in infants which is more prevalent in poor families.

In France for quite a long time, children ages two to six have been going to school. This program is a state-run, tax-financed, *ecole maternelle*. Since their beginning in 1882, these "maternal schools" have become a necessary part of the child's development. While attendance is voluntary, nearly 100 percent of children ages three to six attend as well as many two-year olds. Since it isn't compulsory, the maternal school has become the basis of the school system. This "early" learning for children is the most important time in the child's life for significant mental development.

Other Programs: Health Start, a program in Hampton, VA, came up with more than a million dollars in grants that offered women assistance as soon as they became pregnant. Candidates were asked to complete a family stress check list involving the parents' history and attitudes. A qualifying score made available everything from nutrition to parenting classes with home visits by trained workers. After the child is born, parents join a network of supportive programs designed for all levels of income.

Grandmothers: The Census Bureau reported in June 1999 that there were 3.9 million grandparents taking care of grandchildren under age 18 in 1997—a rise of 77 percent since 1970. Over 5 percent of all children are living with a grandparent due to rising divorce rates, teen pregnancy, child abuse and parents in prison. The 1997 Census Bureau reported that the social consequences for these children include a greater chance they will be raised in poverty, lack health insurance and live in a household that receives public assistance. The report stated 7.7 percent of American children—about 5.5 million—lived with a grandparent. Three-quarters of those were in homes headed by grandparents, continuing a 30-year rise. About 60 percent who are raising children alone are poor, according to the report, and 25 percent are poor even in the households where parents are present.

Helping Pregnant Teens

Pregnant teens have a variety of problems that often affect the infant in devastating ways. An unplanned pregnancy, which is most often the case with teenage mothers, usually involves an unhealthy diet, anxiety, depression, abuse from the infant's father and then desertion. Relief is often sought with alcohol and drugs. This is a time that is the most important not only for the pregnant teen, but for the fetus as well.

The Family Resources Coalition (FRC): The main task of the research done by the Family Resource Coalition involves programs that have worked successfully with pregnant teenagers. These programs operated in a variety of areas. Some operate on their own, others are sponsored by churches, hospitals, schools, day-care-centers, or colleges and universities. Specific program content and structure are determined by the needs of the families being served, and are designed to complement already existing community services and resources.

Most family support programs include:

• Life skills training, including family literacy, education, employment or vocational training, or enhancement of personal development skills such as problem solving, stress reduction and communication.

• Parent information classes that provide instruction in child development and opportunities for parents to share their experience with other parents.

• Parent-child groups and family activities to enable parents to spend more time with their children.

- Crisis intervention and family counseling to respond to parents' special concerns about their children or specific family issues.
- Individual home visitation which focuses on parenting skills, nutrition and early childhood development.
- Early childhood development screening offered when a child is three months and six months old, and thereafter at six month intervals.
- Program staff training once a month for a minimum of two years. The staff attends sessions on teaching parenting skills as well as child development. Trainers use home videos of parent-child infractions to teach home visitors, and as a basis for discussing attachment and strengthening the parent-child relationship. See Appendix B for further information.

Planned Parenthood, Action Fund Inc., has a long term program to help in family planning for the poor, and works diligently against legislation "designed to erode access to reproductive health care and our right to choose." One of their main concerns involves the religious groups who wish "to advance their religious-based views on family planning and abortion."

In their news letter they pointed out that "Every summer, as Congress prepares the budget for the next fiscal year, we encounter an onslaught of amendments designed to undercut or defund support for family planning services to the poor and uninsured. Every year, we must fight amendments that remove guarantees to patient confidentiality, or amendments that would prohibit offering information or services to teens. And, of course, there is the infamous 'gag' rule, which cuts funding for international family planning programs that dare to mention choice; *and is re-introduced each year.*

"If they succeed, there will be virtually no barriers preventing them from enacting their extremist agenda: to eliminate sex education in schools, to eliminate support for family planning, to outlaw abortion, and to close down Planned Parenthood." For more information write to Gloria Feldt, President, Planned Parenthood, 810 Seventh Avenue, New York, NY 10019. Those people opposed to abortion should volunteer to raise the unwanted infants, thus preventing abortions; or should these people continue the prevention of abortion and have the mother raising the unwanted, disliked offspring? The damage done to the child's life and well being in nearly every case is a major crime. What has the most serious consequences—the abortion, or a child's entire life without motherly love, and the painful existence that often results even after the child's adoption?

Even Start: The slogan of this California program is, "Building on existing resources to help parents and children learn together." The program operates out of a grant from the government, and within five years is usually relying on community funds via donations from interested businesses. Initial research on the program, has been good, and its finesse is that it involves the people within the communities in the project to improve their schools and neighborhoods.

The children range in age from infant on and attend preschool or grade school. Mothers and fathers learn about child growth and development, nutrition and family planning. Parents are taught to read and write, fill out a job application, and how to feed a family on a minimum-wage income. Many of the parents who cannot read or write either Spanish or English become literate in both languages. Unfortunately, the program hasn't received the publicity or income it deserves. In California call (916) 657-5218.

Head Start is also a program that appears to be working to some extent. A program of preschool preparation for low income children, Head Start, has existed for over twenty-five years. The elder President Bush requested a $500 million increase in Head Start funding to make the program available to 70 percent of the nation's disadvantaged four-year olds. The program's guidelines were developed by experts in pediatrics, public health, nursing, education, and child development.

Congress has authorized a program, the Child and Family Resource Program, Head Start's early family support program, which provided a choice of services to families and children from birth to age eight. Congress authorized a similar program for children up to the age of five under the title of Comprehensive Child Development Centers. Another example of this approach is the new Head Start Transition Project which provides children in the early school grades with coordinated health, dental, nutritional, and social services similar to those of the Head Start Program.

The Office of Educational Research and Improvement in the US Department of Education has a wide variety of information available on helping single parents raise children successfully. Partnership for Family Involvement in Education, a joint endeavor of the US Department of Education and more than 700 families, education, community, religious, and business organizations, is dedicated to developing family-school-community partnerships. For more information call 1-800-USA-LEARN or the National Library of Education (800) 424-1616.

While there are a variety of programs to alleviate teen pregnancies, unless parents become actively involved, these programs will slowly wither away. Government personnel will make speeches about helping the poor, teenagers, and infant care, but any quick look at the past record of concerned action would find few effective efforts from our elected officials. Unplanned and unwanted infants often suffer lives that are far from pleasant and often tragic.

Curbing Teen-pregnancy

Many students want to learn about sex. A national poll found three fourths wanted to learn how to protect themselves from AIDS, two thirds expressed a desire for information about sexually transmitted diseases, and 58 percent wanted to learn how to deal with pressure to have sex. HIV and herpes have escalated as problems for students and others. The bottom line, however, is that the teenagers

183

must understand all the ramifications of early sex. When they do, teen pregnancy drops. Schools should be able to teach students about sex, all the dangers, all the consequences, and the requirements necessary to raise a healthy child.

The polls have found that most parents do not discuss sex related issues. A national random sample found that the kids between eight to twelve wanted information on these subjects. The survey found that most of the parents of children ages eight to twelve talked about sex only when the children asked the questions. Of course, the main problem with parents is they are afraid if they raise the subject—SEX—it will encourage their children to become interested and experiment. This is the assumption that the children live in a padded cell totally mute on the subjects of most interest to their age groups. Schools must help students learn about the subjects of greatest interest to them, not the age-old school curriculum. Can you imagine what our ancestors will say a hundred years from now because we allowed children to learn about sex on their own when they had little to no knowledge about the sexual transmission of diseases, the danger to the fetus with alcohol and drug consumption, and a total absence of understanding how to help an infant grow and develop a healthy body and an active brain?

Studies have shown that sex education in schools can promote safer sex while actually decreasing sexual experimenting in teenagers. When the basics were presented from condom usage to pregnancy, the results were positive in sex reduction. Adolescents not yet sexually active who receive information about HIV have their first sexual experiences later in life and have fewer sex partners than students who receive HIV information after they have begun having sex. We need to convince some schools of the benefits of sex education since it is essential that students have information about HIV and other major problems resulting from sexual activity without a full understanding of the consequences.

- New York Governor George Pataki put together a task force on out-of-wedlock pregnancies with a video that warns teen-age boys about the cost of child support and a new infusion of federal welfare aid into the effort.
- Kentucky Governor Paul Patton, after a summit meeting on pregnancy prevention, began a $1 million media campaign with the message: Get a Life First.
- In the District of Columbia where two out of three births are to single mothers, the Mayor, Marion Barry, appointed a panel to devise solutions.
- The Outreach Program (TOP) started in St. Louis nearly twenty years ago has since spread to 120 school rooms in 25 cities with good results. TOP changes the children's view of themselves and points out they have a role in the community. When they learn to take care of others, they learn to take care of themselves.

The National Campaign to Prevent Teen Pregnancy seeks to cut teen pregnancy rates by one-third by 2005 by supporting stronger messages on values and a broad array of community-based anti-pregnancy programs. A survey released by the government in May 1997 indicated a decline in the number of teenagers of both sexes who acknowledged having intercourse between the ages of 15 and 19. This successful reduction in teenage pregnancies would be a benefit to all concerned.

Some local schools are doing their part with seventh and eighth graders learning about the issues of sexuality and family life in health education. There is a big push for programs that teach abstinence as the only absolute pregnancy prevention.

Some schools utilize teenage mothers and pregnant girls, some of them as young as age 14 when they had their children. They talked to the teenagers in school as they held their babies. It appears to have a positive affect on reducing teen pregnancies. Controlling teen-age pregnancy will be very difficult and continue to cost American taxpayers extraordinary amounts of support money. The successful programs have come from schools, parent groups, community service agencies, Planned Parenthood affiliates, hospitals, health and family planning clinics, churches, and research organizations, working individually or together in the interests of youth.

Fathers: A program in Los Angeles called L. A. Dads, funded as a one-year pilot program with a $724,000 grant, worked successfully in teaching boys how to care for infants. They were taught how to read to the youngsters, hold them, and work to bond the father to the infant early on. The primary goal was to change the father from seeking recognition in a street gang to earning respect through working with his child. The girls should know and understand both the rewards and consequences of childbirth. The school classes for teen mothers I have attended were primarily for learning child care skills — feeding and changing diapers.

Abusing the Fetus: While protecting the fetus from drug exposure has not been a major topic in our society, it may finally be facing a change. While South Dakota had enacted legislation some time ago, the Wisconsin legislature recently passed a law that could result in a pregnant woman being "detained," and puts exposed fetuses under the jurisdiction of the juvenile courts. In 1995 South Dakota's governor signed into law a bill making it legal to commit substance abusers involuntarily for nearly the entire period of their pregnancy, but in 1997 seven bills were introduced in different states and not passed. Twelve states have introduced similar legislation.

The answer from many "legal experts," is Roe Vs Wade, the abortion case that gave the woman a choice in abortion. While many can agree with abortion, the parents' right to abandon the fetus, the mother's "right" to abuse the fetus with alcohol and drugs, then bear the child, who endures a life of mental and physical disability in social and emotional agony until death, is criminal. So far the courts have considered this a social issue, and want more legislative direction, but as Kathleen Blatz, chief justice of the Minnesota Supreme Court, said, "We keep looking at how to help the child after it's born. What good does that do to anybody?"

In California, a bill to define drug use in pregnancy as criminal abuse failed to pass. Even when the legislation was described, not as infringing on the rights of the woman who takes the drugs, but on helping the child, it still didn't pass. If those who are against legislation to protect these children are so sure of the feminine rights to abuse the fetus, then let them take care of the children who are born to these drug abusing, pregnant women for a year or two; or even to just observe them in our schools as we psychologists do, or in jails and other institutions. A required course in every school should be the dangers of pregnancy, how to avoid them, and raising children.

Curbing Violence and Crime

Violence: The American Psychological Association has traced the origins of juvenile violence to parental rejection or abuse, violence between parents and harsh physical discipline. Children learn violent behavior at home, and the lessons are reinforced by the glorification of violence in the media—also by guns and drugs in our inner cities where young people have been recruited into drug markets in areas the police find difficult to protect. A recent experiment in Kansas City, MO, reduced crime in some areas by 50 percent after police started confiscating illegal guns.

A parent program to curb delinquency has repeatedly shown efficacy for reducing antisocial behaviors and appears to be among the most promising. Two experiments in Eugene, Oregon, demonstrated that teaching parents better monitoring and more consistent roles in discipline techniques reduced school students' violent behaviors. One conclusion was that parenting skills should be taught in high school. Another was that family intervention is difficult and rarely attempted. The most common kinds of programs, counseling by social workers, peer mediation, and neighborhood anti-violence initiatives, are seldom examined to see if they produce lasting benefits.

Many researchers, as a result, are frustrated that the Violent Crime Control Law and Law Enforcement Act of 1994 put most of its $6.1 billion for crime prevention in untested and controversial programs such as "midnight basketball" and other after-school activities. Delbert S. Elliott of the University of Colorado's Center for the Study and Prevention of Violence reported, "The evidence for programs that focus on family relationships and functioning, particularly on family management and parenting practices, is quite strong and consistent." After a study of 450 prevention programs, Elliott "(D)escribed conflict resolution training, peer counseling and peer mediation as ineffective when implemented alone: only when used as part of a more comprehensive prevention approach did they show positive results" (1).

It seems imperative that parents organize anti-violence committees to promote this concept in their local schools, since the programs in most schools do little, if anything, that effectively reduces the violence. The goal can be reached, but it requires more than a metal detector. It involves dealing with the violence that occurs outside of school as well as the behavior on school grounds. Violence can be reduced when group counseling examines the participants, causes for and results from behaviors. For example, the US Department of Education in its booklet "America Goes Back to School," Partners' Activity Kit (1996-97), Partnership for Family Involvement in Education, provided some main areas where violence could be restricted:

- Conflict resolution workshops teach children how to respond without violence when someone is bothering them. Get students involved with an anti-violence campaign.

- Encourage your local paper to cover positive stories about youth activities and accomplishments. Highlight youth, school, and community efforts that have taken on violence, drug, alcohol, and gang issues. Our news media appears to cater to the sensational crime stories while neglecting the news of kindness and consideration. This is because our public appears to be more interested in sensationalism in the form of gang killings, parents murdering their children, and other violent behaviors over good news.

- Create alternative activities to gangs such as performing arts, opportunities in music, dance and theater, sports and community service opportunities.

The booklet *Strong Families, Strong Schools: Building Community Partnerships for Learning* (US Department of Education) states that aggressive behavior in young children is related to later misconduct. Connecting children in positive ways early on with the family and community is important for violence prevention. Some programs that have made a difference were the Perry Preschool Project in Michigan; the Parent-Child Development Center in Houston, Texas; the Family Development Research Project in Syracuse, New York; and the Yale Child Welfare in New Haven, Connecticut. Their common feature was dealing with low-income and often minority families. Each program intervened during the first five years of a child's life and followed up for two to five more years. They combined family involvement and parent training with preschool education for the child. Home visits were a component in each. These programs produced less fighting, impulsiveness, disobedience, restlessness, cheating, and delinquency among children (2). The key is family involvement.

Reducing Poverty

Our democratic society has virtually ignored programs that would help relieve long-term poverty. Each member of the family needs to understand the qualities in learning necessary to function in our society in employment and financial gains. Until children in low income areas receive this economic motivation, our society will remain deeply divided between the rich and middle income people, and the poor.

One solution described in the US Department of Education's "Community Update" issue for July/August 1999 involved the Philadelphia Futures program which is "(D)edicated to improving life opportunities for low-income young people through education. Their center-piece program, Sponsor-A-Scholar (SAS), has enjoyed extraordinary success in the Philadelphia area with 94 percent of SAS students enrolled in college immediately after high school graduation and 88 percent returning for their second year of college."

The program involved both long-term one-on-one mentoring, a financial incentive for college expenses and academic enrichment and support. Different agencies were mobilized including colleges and universities to become involved with city schools. "More than 467 students participate in SAS/Philadelphia, representing more than 50 colleges and universities." The SAS model has been adapted in 10 different programs across the country serving "more than 550 students with mentors, financial incentives, and academic support." For more information on this program, call Debra Kaha at (215) 790-1666 or e-mail philaf@philadelphiafutures. org.

Reducing Drug Usage

A recent survey revealed that many parents are unaware of their children's use of drugs, and/or the consequences that happens to the children who use drugs. The Partnership for a Drug-Free America did a survey and found, that while parents are aware of the drug problem, they do not think of their own children as having a serious problem of exposure to drugs, or that drugs are widely available in their children's schools. The survey included 9,712 children across the nation, and also found that drug use was much lower among children who learn about the risks of drugs at home. Only 28 percent of the children said they learned a great deal about drugs from their parents. On the other hand, 94 percent of the parents surveyed said they talked with their sons and daughters about drugs over the last year. Only 67 percent of the children recalled those discussions. Twenty-one percent of the parents said they believed their children might have tried marijuana, while 44 percent said they had actually tried it. If the parents fail to engage in motivated discussions of the dangers of drug abuse, then the schools must. It is a problem that needs to be directly addressed by both groups.

Unfortunately, the bottom line is that a majority of teenagers say they don't believe there is any risk in trying methamphetamine once or twice. A poll indicated 58% of teenagers in Los Angeles and 56% nationally did not believe that trying methamphetamine posed a big risk. About nine percent of the students nationwide reported they had used the drug, speed, with the number increasing. Nationally 53 percent of drug users were age 15 or under. Methamphetamine is readily available in Southern California from both " . . . Small-time home labs and big manufacturing operations hidden in desert areas, officials said" (3).

"Prevention programs reach less than half the nation's school children, and many of the programs that are used do not adequately cover the key elements of prevention. Moreover, most programs do not provide booster sessions to reinforce important prevention skills during high school, when peer pressure greatly intensifies. Prevention does not work in isolated doses: it must begin early and be repeated regularly." Research suggests normative education is essential in prevention, and provides developmentally appropriate material and activities, including information about the short-term effects and long-term consequences of alcohol, tobacco and illegal drugs. Teaching techniques, such as role playing, discussion, brainstorming and cooperative learning are included along with the necessary prevention elements in at least ten sessions a year (with a minimum of three to five booster sessions in two succeeding years). Teacher training and support is a major part as is an active family involvement. The material is easy for teachers to implement and is culturally relevant for students (3).

Project Alert and Life Skills, which teaches seventh through ninth graders the social skills to help avoid and reduce peer pressure to take drugs, have been given credit for being successful. A Rand study which involved 7,600 students evaluated some programs in 1993 and 1995. This involved 86 schools with 30 in California and Oregon. The results included a reduction in the use of marijuana, reduction of the use of cocaine by 2.9 percent of users, with the benefits outweighing the costs such as crime, lost workplace hours or deaths. The prevention program is far less expensive than treating drug abusers, and the program could be implemented in all middle schools for $500 million.

The PSAC groups could organize programs to help parents explain to their children the dangers of drugs in detail with everything from videos to AA shelter visits. Most parents warn children about drugs, but seldom offer graphic descriptions of what it's like to be hooked on drugs. One visit to a drug re-hab unit would make most children very wary of drug use. Many anti-drug-use groups get volunteers from drug re-hab organizations who are quite willing to relate their stories for the sake of helping others avoid the same mistakes.

A thirty-seven year-old friend of mine who has been fighting drug and alcohol addiction since the age of eleven, is quite willing to tell children about the destruction it can cause in one person's life. One of the interesting and most depressing results of his drug usage for so long a period of time is that it kept him from learning social interaction with others due to being "out of it" because of the drugs.

See Appendix B for some prevention programs, addresses and internet sources.

A study recently released by bipartisan drug experts indicates medical treatment for drug addiction works just as well as treating other physical problems such as diabetes, and is a lot less expensive than the jail time we now supply as a "cure." The federal government spends $17 billion on a drug control budget but only one-fifth of that to treat addicts. A doctors' group indicated this should be increased.

- " The cost for a jailed addict reaches $25,900 per year. Patient drug treatment costs $1,800 with intensive outpatient care at $2,500, and residential drug programs cost $4,400 to $6,800.
- Drug treatment can cut crime by 80 percent according to Brown University addiction director, Norman Hoffman.
- Every dollar invested in drug treatment programs can save $7 in societal and medical costs" (4).

Only about 15 percent of people who need treatment actually get it. Very few states provide any methadone clinic treatment and every US methadone clinic has a waiting list. But even worse, as presented earlier, very few pregnant drug addicts can get treatment because of the lack of sufficient treatment programs, and the inability for the patient to pay. Why is it we can not treat our own people who need help, especially when it involves the lives of the children from pregnant women who are addicted? Are we afraid we'll be accused of promoting addiction rather than condemning it? Shouldn't we work on the cure for addiction long before we spend large amounts on an expensive punishment? Children deformed mentally and physically by mothers' drug addiction are a disaster in our schools with behaviors that in many cases are totally uncontrollable. The lives these children lead are devoid of nearly all the pleasures and worthwhile social experiences other children find daily. Why isn't treatment a priority?

A Sixty Minutes TV program on January 3, 1999, dealt with the drug problem in Zurich, Switzerland. A previous program had investigated open drug use in a public park condoned by the Swiss government with the idea that it would remove the illegality of drug use.

Instead, the park turned over to drug users was strongly avoided by the regular population because of the filth and danger.

A new Swiss program changed drug usage into a medical problem with drugs available from two hospital units twice a day for $10, plus needles. The users praised the program, as did the police for the reduction of crime to obtain expensive drugs. The medical personnel praised it for treating addiction as a biological problem rather than a choice problem. Many of the women gave up prostitution as a means of "earning" drug money, and all agreed that they planned to stop taking drugs.

The doctor who had recommended the Swiss medical approach was asked, "But isn't this a method to cure the drug users that will never get them cured, off the drugs?" The doctor answered, "We treat diabetics every day, and we have no hope of ever curing the patients of their diabetes. The same is true of the drug addicts, but we do treat the problem to reduce other antisocial behaviors." Couldn't we try this?

Reducing the Dropout Rate

> The will to learn is an intrinsic motive, one that finds both its source and its reward in its own exercise. The will to learn becomes a "problem" only under specialized circumstances like those of a school where a curriculum is set, students confined, and a path fixed.
>
> Jerome Brunner, *THE WILL TO LEARN.*

When children find it possible to remain in school to receive an education in *their* interests, school will have more meaning. When schools stop the coercion and punishment game and shift over to creating learning that involves the students, the dropout rate will also be reduced. The primary goal in dropout reduction is to make education interesting to every individual entering the school, including the teachers. When the frustration, humiliation and coercion are eliminated, dropouts in the fourth through the tenth grades will decline, and children will find school rewarding as opposed to compulsory, dull, and demeaning. Children know when teachers and others think they can't learn.

"The problem is that at least half of all students are making little or no effort to learn, because they don't believe that school satisfies their needs. To make school harder — to increase the length of the school year or the school day, to assign more homework, to require more courses in science and mathematics — is not going to reach those students. It's only going to increase the separation between the half who are already working and the half who are not." (4) Most of these dropouts come from the low income, urban schools.

The teaching priority for children should begin with the child's interest(s) and abilities over subject matter, with an emphasis on the teacher understanding the benefits of positive discipline over coercion in learning. A peer review for teachers who lack success in helping students is needed which would result in improvement in teaching skills with peer teacher help. As long as some children feel school attendance is uninteresting, difficult and threatening, the dropouts will continue to increase in number. There are some teachers who make learning exciting and interesting.

Promoting Participation in Democracy

> Without popular information, or the means of acquiring it, is but a prologue to a farce or a tragedy . . . A people who mean to be their own governors must arm themselves with the power which knowledge gives."
>
> James Madison 1751—1836

Increasing voter participation in our democratic programs will be very difficult since our democracy has shifted from the electorate of the masses to the influential groups with subsidies for the candidates. In the elections of 1996 the Hispanic vote was the biggest ever.

But even so, less than half of the voters eligible to vote did so in the Clinton-Dole race. About 95.8 million voters cast a ballot out of 196.5 million who were eligible according to Curtis Gans, director of the Committee for Study of the American Electorate. This was the lowest voter turnout since 1924.

Voter participation in our government will not increase until the citizens understand why their vote is important, and this will not occur until schools teach students that democracy must be protected against a take over by control groups, as has happened in so many other, formerly democratic, countries. These students should also be taught that a democratic government just doesn't happen; it takes effort by the populace to keep informed in order to understand complex legislative issues, as well as the ability to comprehend election battles that often bring out the worst in each candidate, seldom the best.

Schools should become more democratic, increasing as the students progress through the grades with seniors having a large part in voting on school functions, activities, and, perhaps, subject matter in the curriculum. Without a major effort to have our school children become involved in our democratic process, we will continue as a nation to have "elected" officials sponsored by political action committees (PAC) and influence peddlers with the funds to insure election. Those members of our democracy who have the least influence and need it the most, those in low income areas, have virtually no significant representation in their government.

According to Common Cause (1997), "Political action committees (PACs) gave nearly $200 million to congressional candidates—a new record. Special-interest contributions to the parties totaled an estimated $250 million. PAC and special-interest contributions led to a near record 95 percent re-election rate for incumbents. Special-interest PAC 'investments' are rigging our elections and corrupting our Congress." There are loopholes purposely drilled by Congress to get around the limit on political contributions. The buying of an office is becoming a common part of our democratic process. In 1998 the Democrats received $24.1 million in soft-money gifts, a 130 percent increase over their collections two years previously. GOP committees had an increase of 26 percent to $28.3 million.

One major attempt to increase student participation in the community is called Civil Education, a ten-year program fostered by 40 leading educational and social service groups, and The Partnering Initiative on Education and Civil Society. These groups include the NEA, Department of Education, National Association of Independent Colleges and Universities, and the Association of School Administrators. The groups, which represent more than 106,000 schools and universities with 64 million students, will designate 10,000 schools as models for involving students in a range of social service activities like food drives, environmental projects and work with the elderly. The organizers eventually hope to involve up to 16,000 school districts and 3,600 colleges and universities. Parent-School Advisory Committees should check this out for help in their own school districts. It appears these people are on the right track by involving the students in community affairs as the lead-in to political awareness.

If voter participation doesn't increase and PAC influence decrease, the "government of the few" will continue to evolve, and democracy as we know it will be even more distorted. The goals for schools from our elected representatives are an indication of representation—better and higher test scores for promotion to the next grade and for graduation and stronger standards. We need to convince those in the low income schools and neighborhoods of the vital necessity to become involved in the democratic process, and interested in voting. If we don't. . . .

Project Vote Smart is an organization that provides answers to questions on nearly any phase of voting, particularly confusing ballot issues, candidates, and other difficult to understand issues on any state ballot. These questions will be answered by a mixture of party members, Republican and Democrat and others who will mail out information on candidates, propositions, and other phases of knowledge to help the voter. "Information is made easily available to every American free of charge by simply picking up a phone and calling one of the hundreds of trained volunteers and student interns on our toll-free Voter's Research Hotline, or through our Vote Smart Web cite and publications. . . .

"We founded this basic principle of self-governance that is now being emulated the world over. Yet here, in the very heart of democracy, the self-serving manipulation of political campaigns has shattered the citizen's ability to obtain the kind of factual, useful information essential to success, leaving power to those who purchase special access. Not once in the decades of big money, powerful contributors, political posturing and self-serving commercialism has any group challenged this malignancy —UNTIL NOW!" This group, the "Voter's Self-Defense System," adds, "We help teachers make politics come to life in high school classrooms and provide scholarships to college students throughout the country, enabling them to work and study at Project Vote Smart." The first names out of 35 on the first page under Founders of Vote Smart were Barry Goldwater, George McGovern, Mark Hatfield, Bill Bradley along with Geraldine Ferraro and William Proxmire. These are a mixture of both Democrat and Republican supporters. Bill Moyers and David Broder were also included.

Vote Smart/ Center for National Independence in Politics, 129 NW 4th St., #204, Corvallis, OR 97330 or (541) 754-2747 or website WWW.vote-smart.org.

Also the Voter's Research Hotline at 1-888-868-3762.

This is a very important issue in our society—an approach to make voting an important concern for all SES groups.

Some Questions to Ask

1. What is the percentage of "at risk" children in your school? What percentage of families in your community could use HIPPY or PAT programs?

2. Is there a community program for helping pregnant teens—one to check absent fathers?

3. How does your community rate in voter participation in local, state and federal elections?

4. What is the voting record of the 18—24 year old group to evaluate the most recent out-of-school voting people? How does your school promote voting?

5. How does the school funding compare between the low income communities and the affluent ones? What is the per pupil amount, and how is it spent in each school?

6. Do the students in your school vote on anything of significance? Is your school more authoritarian than democratic?

7. How serious is the drug problem? Is the emphasis on curing users or punishing them?

8. Does your school have a program to help prevent or reduce drop-outs?

9. How does your school deal with drug abusers and other substances—alcohol?

10. What are the positive and negative characteristics of your school?

Community Learning Centers (CLC)

> In the normal development of the child, it is now known that, most of the time, if he is given a really free choice, he will choose what is good for his growth. This he does because it tastes good, feels good, gives pleasure or delight. . . . It is necessary in order for children to do well that adults have enough trust in them and in the natural process of growth, i.e., not interfere too much, not make them grow or force them into predetermined design, but rather let them grow and help them grow in a Taoistic rather than an authoritarian way."
>
> Abraham Maslow, *Towards a Psychology of Being*
> 1999, N.Y., J. Wiley & Son

The purpose of a learning center would be to provide learning experiences for those in the community from infants to grandparents in subjects and areas they find interesting. Before your community learning center can be organized, a decision must be made as to how it will be done. One choice involves making it part of the schooling process funded by vouchers, fees, and, most likely, a battle with the school system because of the competition, or separate from school. The second choice can include an after-school CLC that will interest the children far more than school does, and include interest areas for all ages.

If the program is to have an enduring impact, it must influence the child's behavior outside of school as much as in class. Second, a school classroom does not lend itself to many of the kinds of informal activities involving parents, other adults, and older children. Accordingly, some kind of neighborhood center becomes a desirable feature for a comprehensive learning program. Such a center should be open after school, on weekends, and during vacations with staff members on duty. The center should be represented to the community not merely as a place where children go, but rather where all members of the community gather in the joint interest of themselves and their children. Thus, Community Learning Centers that encourage exploring children's interests will find children coming back regularly to pursue their interests more often.

CLC's would provide the following:
• Encouragement of community cohesion, cooperation and allegiance.
• More parental involvement in children's education.
• More child interest in learning and increased self esteem.
• Cultural and community language centers to meet the child's and parents' needs.
• A source of help for parents to understand the needs of children and how to meet those needs.
• Development of creative activities for children as an alternative to gang violence, crime and lack of interesting activities.

Advantages:

1. The elimination of the Hidden Curriculum is, no doubt, the greatest advantage for the adoption of the CLC, along with the opportunity for children to learn and relate to that learning. It could remove the crushing loss of self esteem and self worth inflicted upon children each day they are in coercive schools, and provide an opportunity for children to reach and even surpass their potential.

2. A CLC could also eliminate the present false goals of schooling and replace them with the needs of each learner — no grades, no tests beyond those required by the learner and not a teacher to find out where the learner was in relation to the teacher's goals. There would be no retention, flunk, failure, retarded or special ed. classes, detention, humiliation, permission to go to the toilet, dress codes, or a prison-like atmosphere. If a facilitator or a child do not agree, each could say good-by, or "let's try again." The learner could leave without recrimination or a great deal of stress.

3. CLC's could be financed by the local community, by vouchers, by tax deductions from parents who do not send their children to public schools, or by grants—or all of the above. Many of the facilitators would, it is assumed, work to help out, and would volunteer their services rather than work for pay.

4. CLC's would again involve the children in the community, dealing with real people rather than TV images or screen idols. Visits to offices, schools, and campaigners for office could help bring about the reality seldom found in a classroom.

5. The hypocrisy of schooling and the adulation of the false gods of grades, test scores, and rote memory could be replaced by the reasoned aims and goals of each individual learner—which could be getting a good job, how to drive, draw, roller skate, or passing the SAT or other long-term goals. The CLC committee could come up with more specific rules, regulations and interest areas based on their knowledge and understanding of the community interests and needs.

Today in our society the transition into "adulthood" has deteriorated into a graduation program not attended by one-fourth or more of the students who either dropped out or were pushed out. In order to re-establish democracy in each community and to make adolescence meaningful, we must involve the youth of today in the community process. The premise is that learning can take place in a variety of situations, not just in a school, as has been shown by innumerable studies.

Large numbers of parents will not abandon the public schools and rush to the learning centers for their children's' learning. On the other hand, it is quite apparent that a significant number of parents are thoroughly disenchanted with the public schools, and are searching for an alternative to the present inefficient learning process.

The CLC would be operated by a few paid personnel, who would be responsible for the operation of the center from ordering materials (films, TV's, CD's, books, toilet paper, heating supplies, plumbing, upkeep, etc.) helping to locate volunteers, facilitators and network personnel. The facilitators would be available by phone to help the learner gain knowledge about a dance, sea anemone, plumbing, computers, via many of the avenues of learning such as the library, internet, experts, visits to the location, etc. These knowledgeable people would volunteer to help learners in the CLC, as well as other members of the community, parents and students, who would be available to help out, and participate in discussions, dancing or daydreaming. These CLC activities would be the result of the interest of children and adults.

Objections to the CLC's would come from those who equate learning with a teacher, a trained teacher who is credentialed. This, of course, is part of the schooling mythology. Learning in no way equates with a teacher, and this is not to demean those excellent teachers who inspire some children some of the time. Most of what we have learned, all of us, comes from our experiences, not with a teacher, but on our own with those Carl Rogers called, "significant others." We learn best from models we respect and with whom we can relate. Uri Bronfenbrenner, the author of *Children Teach Children: Learning by Teaching*, pointed out that children learn from older children they respect and the tutors themselves benefit as much, if not more, than the tutored. In CLC's children could help one another to learn by suggesting, imitating, and watching, or by simply helping out. The centers could be staffed by people who enjoy what they are doing, older children, parents without children, grandparents and those who enjoy being around the spontaneity of children.

In the CLC's children would learn to read at their own interest with the help of those who can make their learning as a pleasurable experience, not as an exercise in accomplishing a skill on a test that exceeds a spurious norm so the child will be reading "above grade level," thus reflecting the teacher's accomplishment, not the student's.

Not all children would benefit from CLC's. My experience as a psychologist in public schools with compulsory attendance has shown that with some learners there is a built-in need for structure. These children have a need to be told what to do, monitored to see that they do it, and given the token rewards that schools utilizes to reinforce good behavior. This results from a lack of experience in freedom and choice and/or the opportunity to explore and learn on their own. These children generally come from authoritarian families in which the parents demand obedience to rules, regardless of the logic of the rules ("You'll do it because I said so!"). Their families are generally associated with restricted curiosity, originality and fancifulness. The children raised in families with authoritative parents are more aggressive, more anxious, and lack controls. Even A. S. Neil in his free school, Summerhill, didn't take every child who wanted to enter. He was very much aware that some just could not handle freedom. For these children raised in an authoritarian environment, public schools are the most convenient answer. Check out Neil's book, *Summerhill*.

After-School CLC's: Financing the CLC's will vary from payments for the site and a caretaker, to teaching aids such as the computer internet, TV, and other interesting learning equipment. There are a wide variety of "educational" TV programs that interest children of all ages immediately. President Clinton's 1999 budget proposed $200 million for the 21st Century Community Learning Centers Program—$1 billion over five years—which would provide start-up funds to school-community collaborations across the nation to establish or expand before-and-after school, weekend and summer programs for school-age children. The after-school initiative is part of a $20 billion package over five years to improve child care for America's working families, the largest single investment in child care in the nation's history.

This program will enable schools to stay open during non-traditional school hours, where mentoring in basic skills, enrichment in the core academic subjects, arts and music classes, recreational activities, and drug and violence prevention can take place in a safe and supervised environment. "Every child needs some place to go after school," President Clinton said. "With after-school programs, we can not only keep our kids healthy and happy and safe, we can teach them to say 'no' to drugs, alcohol and crime; 'yes,' to reading, sports and computers." The popularity of the program was evident when 2,000 school systems applied for 286 grants. Call 1-800-USA-LEARN for applications.

The school monopoly would be seriously threatened by CLC's, and objections will come loudly from teacher organizations that have fought the voucher, and school personnel who resent the competition. However, the argument against compulsory attendance and the failure to produce learning in a large segment of the compelled student body will be the factors to convince many parents. Parents do have the right to deal with their children in a variety of ways, which includes sending the children to the learning institution of their choice.

Enjoyment in Learning

> The basic concept of American education has been primarily puritanical—we must learn facts in an atmosphere of overt regimentation that will lift us from bondage into servitude and finally steady employment and marriage, family retirement and death. What is missing is enjoyment, pleasure in learning, hobbies.
>
> Bertrand Russell, *Education and the Good Life* 1926.

Learning about learning is not new. Aristotle believed that the ultimate goal of any true state was to teach the child how life could be enjoyed. In our schools today, enjoyment in learning is the last item on the educational menu. We feel we must "raise standards" to force children to learn what they don't want to by threatening them with failure and repetition of the same grade if they don't relinquish their interests to those in control and learn what is required. Does this make sense? Why is doing well on a test made by an outsider and accompanied by threats of failure, social humiliation, and grade repetition if the student doesn't score well, the most important evaluation of student learning?

The main goal in life for most American people as promoted by our society, our religions, and our schools is a diploma to enable us to find a job and earn a living. As a result of these standards, we work hard, study to get somewhere, but seldom really enjoy life. Enjoyment, apparently, has not been one of our goals, even though it's talked about a lot. A major goal of school should be to discover and encourage the student's interests and to make learning desirable and a goal for all children on a long-term basis.

We get enjoyment in learning by the same process infants do when they learn to understand the sounds made by those taking care of them, mothers and others. They learn to coordinate their muscles in moving, reaching, and then learn to talk, all on their own which produces smiles and enjoyment for all concerned. Walking is also part of the infant's desire to learn. This desire for learning does not stop when reinforced throughout the child's life. The brain is always looking for new stimulation, and it doesn't take threats, coercion and humiliation to produce effective learning. It takes understanding of the learner's interests and motives. This produces enjoyment in older children just as it does for infants.

When our children receive stimulation in the pursuit of their own interests and find satisfaction in those endeavors, then our society will change. There will be a major decline in the use of drugs, alcohol and other sources of a physical disabling means of "getting high." We will have a major reduction in single parenting and children born with FAS and other disabling medical problems that deny them a healthy and enjoyable life in place of the tortuous existence many experience from day to day in our schools. Our society will change from primarily two separate economic groups, one with enough income and financial strength to provide the pleasures and the other, the lower income families who can barely make it. This will not take place, however, until our schools and society are changed to make equality in education a reality. This equality is possible, but will be achieved only after a massive parental effort. Your help is vital.

REFERENCES

Preface-Introduction

1. Schwebel, Milton, *Who Can Be Educated?* 1968 (p. 5) Schwebel was the dean of the Graduate School of Education at Rutgers University.

2. Friedenberg, Edgar Z., "Requiem for the Urban Schools," *Saturday Review,* Nov. 18, 1967, p77.

Part One

1. Churchman, C. West, *Center Magazine,* November 1978.

2. Fynman, Richard, "Most Experts Don't Know More Than the Average Person," *US News & World Report,* March 18, 1985.

3. Postman, Neil and Weingartner, *Teaching as a Subversive Activity,* 1968.

4. Bonfenbrenner, Urie, *The Two Worlds of Childhood/The US and the USSR,* Russell Sage Publications, 1970.

5. *School Psychology Review,* October 1998, National Assoc. of School Psychologists —NASP.

6. *Communiqué,* A publication of NASP, May 1990.

7. Baer, George G., Kathleen M. Minke, & Alex Thomas, 1997, *Children's Needs II: Development Problems and Alternatives,* NASP.

8. Reich, Charles, *The Greening of America,* 1969.

9. Rogers, Carl, *Freedom to Learn,* Charles Merrill, 1969.

14217-PIER

Part Two

1. Schwebel, Milton *Who Can Be Educated?* p 202, 1968.

2. Quinn, Kevin P. and James I. McDougal, "A Mile Wide and A Mile Deep: Comprehensive Interventions for Children and Youth with Emotional and Behavioral Disorders and Their Families," *School Psychology Review*, Vol. 17, No. 2, 1998, published by National Association of School Psychologists, NASP.

3. "Decline in Special Ed Teachers," *Special EDge*, Summer 1994, California Association of School Psychologists (CASP).

4. Gould, Steven, *The Mismeasurement of Man*, 1981.

Part Three

1. Zill, Nicholas (1990), Child Trends, Inc., Washington, DC, *The Future of the US as a Nation of Readers*, 214 N. Marianne Winglee, John Cabin, MD, Seven Locks Press.

2. Profile of Alcohol and Drug Use During Pregnancy in California 1992. "Perinatal Substance Exposure Study Scientific Report," Health and Welfare Agency, California Department of Alcohol and Drug Programs, Office of Perinatal Substance Abuse, University of California, Berkeley School of Public Health, Western Consortium for Public Health. This study reported on the drug usage of 29,494 pregnant women.

3. Zuckerman, Mortimer, *US News & World Report*, "Changing Times . . . the look for the future," July 18, 1994.

4. National Center for Education Statistics, US Department of Health and Human Services, California Child Care Resource & Referral Network, *Los Angeles Times*, June 27, 1999.

5. Schwebel, Milton *Who Can Be Educated?* 1968

6. Friedenberg, Edgar "Requiem for the Urban Schools," *Saturday Review*, Nov 18, 1967.

Part Five

1. Rosenthal, Robert & Lenore Jacobson, *Pygmalion in the Classroom* Published by Irvington 1989.

Part Six

1. Elliott, Delbert S. "Forestalling Violence," *Scientific American,* September 1998.

2. "Strong Families, Strong Schools: Building Community Partnerships for Learning," US Government Department of Education, September 20, 1999.

3. "Making the Grade: A Guide to School Drug Prevention Programs," from Drug Strategies, 2445 M Street, NW, Suite 480, Washington, DC 20007 (202 663 6090) Fax 202-663-6110

4. Gough, Puline B. The Key to Improving Schools: An Interview with William Glasser, *Phi Delta Kappan,* May 1987.

Education Publications

Most of the following are from the US Department of Education. Call 1-800-USA-LEARN for free information.

- "Strong Families, Strong Schools: Building Community Partnerships for Learning," Sept. 1994.
- "Together We Can: A Guide for Crafting a Profamily System of Education and Human Services," US Department of Education Office of Educational Research and Improvement, April 1993. "This book was developed . . . to help communities improve coordination of education, health and human services for at-risk children and families."
- "New Skills for New Schools: Preparing Teachers in Family Involvement," developed by the Harvard Family Research Project.

- "America Goes Back to School, Partners' Activity Guide."
- "Reaching All Families and Creating Family Friendly Schools."
- "Employers, Families and Education: Promoting Family Involvement in Learning."
- "Get Involved! How Parents and Families Can Help Their Children Do Better in School."
- "Team up for Kids! How Schools Can Support Family Involvement in Education."
- "Be Family-Friendly: It's Good Business."
- "Join Together for Kids! How Communities Can Support Family Involvement in Education."
- "Summer Home Learning Recipes."
- Helping Your Child Learn Series (Reading, Math and Others).
- Partnerships for Family Involvement in Education, 600 Independence Avenue, SW, Washington, DC, 20202-8173, 1-800-USA-LEARN.
- The National Coalition for Parent Involvement in Education, Institute for Educational Leadership, 1001 Connecticut Ave., NW, Suite 310, Washington, DC 20036, (202-822-8405).
- *Urgent Message: Families Crucial to School Reform* which emphasizes the need to include family involvement in school reform efforts. Write to the Center for Law and Education, 1875 Connecticut Avenue, NW, Washington, DC. 20009.
- "Empowerment and Family Support" a Cornell Cooperative Extension publication; a collection of Cornell's magazine publications. Mon Cochran, editor.

Drugs:
- "Growing Up Drug Free, A Parent's Guide to Prevention," US Department of Education, (1-800-624-0100), or write to Growing up Drug Free, Pueblo, CO 81009, or National Clearinghouse for Alcohol and Drug Information, PO Box 2345, Rockville, MD 20852.
- "What Works: Schools Without Drugs," 1-800-624-0100, or write to Schools Without Drugs, Pueblo, CO 81009, or Information Of-

fice, US Department of Education, 555 New Jersey Avenue, NW. Washington, DC 20208.

- "Making the Grade: A Guide to School Drug Prevention Programs," Drug Strategies, 2445 M Street, NW, Suite 480, Washington, DC 20037, (202-663-6090), fax 202-663-6110.

Even Start:

- "Family Support Guidelines for Effective Practice in the Early Intervention Service System for Families of Infants and Toddlers with Disabilities or At Risk."
- California's EARLY START Program, Central Directory of Early Intervention Resources, 1996. A Guide to State and Regional Public Funded Agencies and Resources of California. Call the Early Start Program at 1-800/515 BABY. Early Start Program in California 1-800-894-9799 or 916/641-5925.

Booklets:

- National Education Goals Panel's Handbook for Local Goals Report, "Building a Community of Learners." The National Educational Goals Panel, 1850 M Street, 270, Washington, DC 20036, (202 632-0952).
- "What Works, Research About Teaching and Learning," US Department of Education. Introduction by William J. Bennett, Secretary of Education, US Department of Education.
- Partners in Action: A Resource Guide: Part I, "Six Portraits of Effective Family-School-Community Collaboration." Part II, "Organizations That Serve and Support Family-School-Community Collaboration." Write to the Center on Families, Communities, Schools & Children's Learning, Johns Hopkins University, 3505 North Charles Street, Baltimore, Maryland 21218, (410-516-8800) / 410-516-8890 FAX. Also, an Annotated Bibliography from the same source. "The mission of the Center on Families, Communities, Schools and Children's Learning is to conduct research, evaluation, policy analyses, and dissemination to produce new and use-

ful knowledge about how families, schools and communities influence student motivation, learning, and development. A second important goal is to improve the connections among these social institutions as children proceed from infancy through high school."

PAT, HIPPY

- Parents as Teachers (PAT), 9374 Olive Boulevard, St. Louis, MO 63132, (314-432-4330).
- HIPPY USA, Teachers College, Box 113, 525 West 10th St., New York, NY 10027, (212-678-3500).
- HIPPY Application Form, HIPPY USA, 53 West 23rd St., New York, NY 10010, (212) 645-2006.
- Home Instruction Program for Preschool Youngsters, Theory and Practice (53 West 23rd St., New York, NY 10010, (212) 645-2006)

"Launching a HIPPY Program, A Guide to Fund—Raising" (53 West 23rd St., New York, NY 10010, (212) 645-2006. NY, NY, plus a startup manual.

And More:

- The National PTA, 135 South La Salle, Dept. 1860, Chicago, IL 60674-1860, (312-549-3253), fax 312-477-5818.
- The Consumer Information Center, Dept. 593C, Pueblo, CO 81009.
- An ACCESS Printout on School Dropouts: Problems and Programs, The National Committee for Citizens in Education, 10840 Little Patuxent Parkway, Suite 301, Columbia, Maryland 21044, 1-800 NET-WORK (638-9675).
- Hurt Healing Hope— Caring for Infants and Toddlers in Violent Environments, ZERO TO THREE/National Center for Clinical Infant Programs, 2000 14th Street North, Suite 380, Arlington, VA 22201-2500, (703) 528-4300, fax (703) 528-6848.

- "Empowerment & Family Support," A Cornell Cooperative Extension Publication. This edition included copies of the bulletin Empowerment and Family support from 1989 to Sept. 1991. Cornell Empowerment Project, 283 Martha Van Rensselaer Hall, Ithaca, NY 14853. (607) 255-1820, fax (607) 255-4071.
- *Turning Points: Preparing American Youth for the 21st Century* (8/89). The Carnegie Council on Adolescent Development, Carnegie Corporation of New York. The book deals with teenagers' problems in school and afterwards because of the poor quality of middle and high school education. They recommend a community approach to supplant the large school and class anonymity.

SOME BOOKS OF INTEREST

- Barth, Roland S. *Improving Schools from Within,* Jossey-Bass, 1990. His main point is the poor interpersonal relationship between faculty and administration.
- Bronfenbrenner, Urie, *Two Worlds of Childhood/US & USSR,* Russell Sage Foundation, 1970. Implications indicate great changes are due in our educational system. His research has not been given the attention it deserves.
- Friedenberg, Edgar, *The Vanishing Adolescent,* Beacon Press, 1959. The standard classic on the subjugation of our youth.
- Glasser, William, *Quality Schools.* I attended his seminars . . . good. It's worth your time.
- Goleman, Daniel, *Emotional Intelligence.* A Bantam Book, Oct. 1995. Good.

- Klass, Carol S., 1996, *Home Visiting: Promoting Healthy Parent and Child Development.* Brookes Publishing Company, Edward Zigler, a noted psychologist quoted in this book says, "Carol Klass has given us the definitive manual for the early intervention professional whose visits foster not only healthy development of the child but the parent as well."

  Also from Brookes: *Strengthening the Family-Professional Partnership in Service to Young Children,* also, *Partnerships in Family-Centered Care: A Guide to Collaborative Early Intervention.* "This practical text shows how to implement Part II of IDEA, . . ." Brookes Publishing Co, PO Box 10624, Baltimore, MD 21285-0624, www.pbrookes.com

- Kohl, Herbert, *The Open Classroom,* New York Book Review, 1969. He advocates working within the system, but not with it. A short, easy, interesting book.

- Kozol, Johnathan, *Death at an Early Age,* A serious description of life in a ghetto school . . . and the death of learning.

- Roberts, Richard N., Sarah Rule, Mark S. Innocent (1997). *Strengthening the Family—Professional Partnership in Services for Young Children,* Brookes Publishing Company, November 1997.

- Holt, John, *How Children Fail,* 1964; *How Children Learn,* 1966; *The Underachieving School,* 1969. Pitman Publishing Company.

- Mead, Margaret, *Culture and Commitment. A study of the Generation Gap,* Double Day, 1970. A short, well done view of our changing culture and the school's inability to either change or cope with it.

- Piaget, Jean, *Science of Education and the Psychology of the Child.* Orion Press, NY, 1970. The translation comes out stilted and stuffy, but the ideas are still there.

- Postman, Neil and Charles Weingartner, *Teaching as a Subversive Activity,* Delacorte Press, NY, 1969. They suggest methods to improve education within the system. Fun to read and full of good ideas, especially their "inquiry method."

- Russell, Bertrand, *Education and the Good Life*. Avon Book Division, 1926. His ideas more than a half a century ago read as up-to-date.
- Schwebel, Milton, *Who Can Be Educated?* Grove Press, 1969.
- *Positive Discipline in the Classroom,* Nelsen, Jane, Lynn Lott, and H. Stephen Glenn, 1997, Prima Publishing. "It creates a classroom climate that enhances Academic Learning. . . . Use class meetings and other positive discipline strategies effectively." This should be required reading for all school personnel.
- *Positive Discipline: A Teacher's A-Z Guide,* Jane Nelsen, Roslyn Duffy, Linda Escobar, et al. Very good. These books are a must for teachers. The authors have been putting on seminars that teachers and parents should check out.
- Hirsch, E. D. Jr. *The Schools We Need—And Why We Don't Have Them,* 1996, Doubleday. Hirsch is a noted writer on learning, and gave a 315 page dialogue of the opposite viewpoints presented in this book. The book cover states, "Mainstream research has shown that if children—*all* children, not just the privileged—are taught in ways that emphasize hard work, the learning of facts, and rigorous testing, their enthusiasm for school will grow, their test scores will rise, and they will be come successful citizens in the information-age civilization." His educational philosophy opponent, Sizer, and I both disagree with this "research."

GLOSSARY

ADA: Average Daily Attendance: a system to provide the public schools with money based on the number of pupils who attend that school — so much per pupil. Very often the school population is not known due to transfers, expulsions and absentees, etc.

AD: This label, adjustment disorder, is given to children who have lost a parent either by divorce, death or disappearance, and who respond with extreme behaviors that are difficult to understand. The problem is often thought of as the child's feeling of rejection by the disappearance of the parent, but no doubt other factors are included. The AD child's actions may range from withdrawal to aggressive and destructive.

AFDC: Aid to Families with Dependent Children, usually low income families. Financial assistance to families with children who are having specific learning problems.

APA: The American Psychological Association whose members are psychologists.

ARC: An accountability report card required yearly for some schools in some districts to publish vital statistics such as enrollment, ethnicity, grades, test scores, absentees, dropouts, number of graduates, etc. Some schools give excellent ARC's, others ignore the requirement.

ASAT: Abbreviated Stanford Achievement Test

AT RISK: Children who have little chance at success in school, exhibit irrational behaviors and are problematic in school are labeled "at risk." Most often they are the product of a single parent, from low income areas, and have had little, if any, help in developing social and emotional skills.

CLAS: California Learning Assessment System—dated.

CASP: The California Association of School Psychologists.

CLAS: California Learning Assessment System. A widely used achievement test.

DARE: Drug Abuse Resistance Education. A drug program that has not been too successful in reducing drug use.

DATE: Drug and Tobacco Education. A program for deterring children from drugs and tobacco.

EBD: Emotional Behavior Disorder given to children who have difficulty controlling feelings and anger.

FAS: Fetal Alcohol Syndrome. A physical-mental problem for infants resulting from women drinking alcohol while pregnant, especially in the second and third trimesters. The effect on the infant can range from mild to significant loss of mental abilities and other disabilities.

GPA: Grade point average is usually based on an average of semester grades. This grade average is often combined with the SAT score for college admission.

IEP: Individual Education Program. A program resulting from federal and local legislation (see PL. 94-142) for special ed students determined by a committee of special education personnel, often involving the psychologist who has done the testing and interviews, the resource specialists who is the person in charge of special education in that school, the principal or the agent since principal's often do not attend IEP meetings, the counselor, the child's teacher(s), and parents. This committee decides if the child qualifies for special education, the special education class the child attends, what are the long-term goals for the child, and why the child qualified for special education. These meetings are long, often boring, and provide ego satisfaction for some teachers, parents and psychologists in long winded presentations.

IQ: The intelligence quotient is often derived from one of two major tests; either the Wechsler Intelligence Scale for Children (WISC-III) or the Stanford Binet. The WISC-III gives two major areas of IQ: Verbal IQ and Performance IQ. Significant scores on the WISC-III are: Below 70 is retarded; 70 to 84 = poor, and considered retarded by some; 85 to 115 is average; 116 to 130 good; above 130 superior.

LEA: Local Education Agency. This is an organization formed on the local level to help improve the schools or educational systems often composed of concerned parents. Grants are available in this area.

NAEP: National Assessment of Educational Progress. A test given to assess learning in children and widely used on a national scale.

NAPE: National Assessment of Partnership in Education

NASP: The National Association of School Psychologists. An organization of school psychologists and professors of school psychology.

OJT: On the job training.

PAC: A political action committee, usually made up of influential and/or wealthy individuals or large corporations who contribute money to the candidates they wish to get elected, and in return expect favors for the donations. While this money gathering has been hotly debated in Congress and elsewhere, very little has been done to keep it in check. The reason: elections have become absurdly expensive.

Percentile: In comparison with others who took the same test, the best score in percentile is 99, the worst the first percentile. The average is 50 with the range from about 25 to 75, depending upon what is being measured and the subjects involved. On some tests the 15th percentile is considered low average. The percentile is often demonstrated on a "bell curve," indicating the majority of the scores are bunched into the middle of the bell curve, and only a very few scores are in the outer limits below the 10th percentile and above the 90th.

PSAC: Parent-School Advisory Committee. A committee formed by concerned parents and others to help improve the public schools.

PTSD: Post Traumatic Stress Disorder. A problem found in children who were physically abused, hit, shaken, spanked severely and/or traumatized when very young, causing stress patterns in the child, or subject to severe stress due to parent absence or other stress conditions. The symptoms range from withdrawal to very active aggression.

Public Law 94-142: Significant legislation passed in 1970 to help children with learning disabilities utilize school more successfully. Started in 1975 after some mothers of retarded children protested its delay, it was subsequently added to by current legislation.

Restructuring School: A term used mainly by college and university people in the process of rebuilding, reorganizing and rearranging to improve the total effectiveness of a school.

SAT: Scholastic Aptitude Test. A test required by some colleges and universities for students with sufficient scores to be accepted into the institution. Many schools are rated on how their students do on the SAT, and if they get into college. Revised from the 1997 version with a change in average scores. The high school GPA is often ranked with the SAT score for college admission.

SED: Serious Emotional Disability as defined by PL 94-142 and subsequent legislation was a label given to students with behavioral problems. The definition is long and ambiguous allowing for manipulation by school personnel and parents. It basically describes a child who can not control behaviors, does not respond to therapy, and misreads praise, anger, attention, etc. Since 1997 the term has been changed to Emotional Disability (ED) and ILS (Integrated Life Services).

Special Education: Classes for children who are described by the school and IEP committee as different from the normal student.

That difference may be in learning, behaviors, visual-motor problems, or any one of dozens of labels from autism to Zebra.

SES: Socioeconomic Status refers to the social and income level of the individual or group. Blacks and Hispanics, for example, are most often found in the lower SES groups, but whites make up the largest number of the lower SES population.

SIDS: Sudden Infant Death Syndrome is a cause of death that is not entirely understood, but has possible causes such as the infant being smothered while sleeping on the stomach, birth defects and others dangers including tobacco, etc.

SSI: Supplemental Security Income. Governmental payments as a supplement to AFDC to help families bear the cost of disabled children including emotionally disturbed children. It is now sometimes used by greedy parents who promote irrational behaviors in their children to collect the extra income.

TESTS: ACT: American College Test for college admission.

CLAS: California Learning Assessment System

GRE: Graduate Record Exam; a substitute for a high school diploma by passing the test.

PSAT: Preliminary Scholastic Aptitude Test—a runner up for the SAT, usually taken in the junior year in high school.

SAT: Scholastic Achievement Test given to high school seniors.

SAT-9: The Stanford Achievement Test, 9th edition, known as SAT-9 is published by Harcourt Educational Measurement, and is a national test of "basic skills" given to students in grades two through eleven.

Appendix A

Choosing A School

Here is a "checklist' of questions from the Department of Education Office of Research Improvement, titled "Choosing a School for Your Child," May 1989.

Curriculum:

    1. Thorough coverage of basic subjects? (Yes or No or Why Not?)

    2. A special focus or theme to the curriculum? (If so, what is it?)

    3. Elective offerings (if appropriate)? (Do they fit students' needs?)

    4. Extracurricular programs to enhance learning and character development?

Policies:

    1. Encouragement of attributes of good character?

    2. Discipline? A primary motivator or is there positive reinforcement?

    3. Homework; how much per subject? Homework hotlines?

    4. Tutoring? By whom?

    5. Grades, feedback and recognition? How often? Based on what ability?

    6. Special achievement and honors for the school?

Resources:

    1. Library? Quality? Recent books? Subject matter of concern?

14217-PIER

2. Classroom book for independent reading? Such as —

3. Physical education facilities; girls involved?

Parent involvement:

1. Parent volunteers in the school?

2. Teachers enlisting parent cooperation on home testing?

3. Partnerships with local business or other institutions?

Reputation:

1. Views of parents with children in the school?

2. Views of friends and neighbors?

3. Views of community leaders?

4. Can parents transfer students to another school? Does state law allow this?

Other:

1. Is there a large room or auditorium for special meetings?

2. Are there specialists in art, reading, science, special education, librarians, counselors and teacher aides?

3. Parent activities?

4. Community resources? Guest speakers, local institutions, etc.

APPENDIX B

Help for Pregnant Teens and Family Service Publications.

"Working with Teen Parents," a government publication, describes a variety of agencies working with pregnant teens and children. "Reaching All Families, Creating Family-Friendly Schools" is a good Department of Education pamphlet. "Parents are the essential link in improving American education, and schools simply have to do a better job of reaching out to them."

Teenage Pregnancies: Check out the Publications Catalog, Fall 1998, Substance Abuse and Mental Health Services Administration's (SAMHSA) National Clearing House for Alcohol and Drug Information and order "Children at Risk because of Parental Substance Abuse." OAS Working Paper 11pp RPO965. Use the web site www.health.org, or write to National Clearing House for Alcohol and Drug Information, PO Box 2345, Rockville, MD 20847-2345 or call 1-800-729-6686.

The Family Resource Coalition in Chicago, Illinois has an excellent book, *Working With Teen Parents.* Write to: The Family Resource Coalition, 230 North Michigan Avenue, Suite 1625, Chicago, IL 60601 or phone 312/726-4750. The FRC grew out of Family Focus, was formed in 1982 to share information, and moved to a national level.

14217-PIER

WARMLINE Family Resource Center (FRC), 916/613-7995 for information on Infant Development Programs, 916/942-2155.

Preventing Child Abuse and Neglect Through Parent Education. Early Childhood Education, Blending Theory; Blending Practice, Brookes Publishers, PO Box 10642, Baltimore, MD 21285-0624. www.pbrookes.com

ACCESS—A Service for Pregnant Teens, Family Services of Central Massachusetts, 71 Elm St., Worchester, MA 01609, 617/756-7123.

Addison County Parent/Child Center, Box 646, 11 Seminary St., Middlebury, VT 05753, 802/3883171.

Aunt Martha's Youth Service Center, Young Employment Unit (YEU), 20200 North Ashland, Chicago Heights, IL 60411, 312/755-0387.

The Caring Connection, St. Luke's Memorial Hospital, Inc., 1320 Wisconsin Ave., Racine, WI 53403, 414/636-2479.

Day and Extended Day Program, Crittendon Hasting House, 10 Perthshire Road, Brighton, MA 02135, 617/782-7600.

The Door—A Center for Alternatives, 618 Avenue of the Americas, New York, NY 10011, 212/691-6161.

Family Life Center, The Bridge, 23 Beacon St., Boston, MA 02108, 617/227-7114.

Infant Stimulation/Mother Training Project, University of Cincinnati Medical Center College of Medicine, Department of Pediatrics, 231 Bethesda Ave., Cincinnati, OH 45267, 513/872-5341.

Jessie's Center for Teenagers, 154 Bathurst St., Toronto, Ontario, Canada M5V 2R3, 416/365-1888.

Job Tipps, Boston YMCA, Metropolitan Administration, 140 Clarendon St., Boston, MA 02116, 617/536-7940.

Johns Hopkins Center for Teenage Parents and Their Infants, Johns Hopkins Hospital, Room 307, Park Building, Baltimore, MD 21205, 301/955-2976

Lula Belle Stewart Center, 1534 Webb Avenue, Detroit, MI 48206, 313/867-2372.

Meadowlark House, Inc., 514 West 24th St., Cheyenne, WY 82001, 307/632-7677; 777-7561.

Meld Young Mothers (MYM), Minnesota Early Learning Design, 123 Grant St., Minneapolis, MN 55403, 612/870-4478.

Mother Visitor Program, Family Focus, 2135 North Kenmore Avenue, Chicago, IL 60614, 312/281-5987.

Alan Guttmacher Institute (AGI) 120 Wall St., New York, NY. 10005 212/248-1111, FAX 212/248-1951, or

The National Organization on Adolescent Pregnancy and Parenting, Inc., (NOAPP), 4421-A East-West Highway, Bethesda, Maryland 20841, 301/913-0378.

Advocates for Youth, 1025 Vermont Avenue NW, Suite 200, Washington, DC 20005, 202/347-5700, FAX 202/347-2263.

The Family Resource Coalition, 200 Michigan Ave., 16th Floor, Chicago, IL 60604, 312/341-0900, FAX 312/241-9361.

Drug Prevention Programs: For up-to-date drug prevention information try http://www.health.org/pubs/catalog/data.htm

For information on alcohol and pregnancy try: http://www.health.org/pubs/qdocs /alcohol/fas-broc/index.htm

In California: http//www.adp.cahwnet.gov. for information on alcohol and FAS

Write to the National Clearinghouse for Alcohol and Drug Information, PO Box 2345 Rockville, MD 20847, "Substance Abuse and Mental Health Services Administration (SAMHSA) National Clearing House for Alcohol and Drug Information (NCADI). (This) is the nation's one-stop resource for the most current and comprehensive information about substance abuse prevention. We distribute the latest studies and surveys, guides, video cassettes, and other types of information and materials on substance abuse from various agencies such as the US Departments of Education and Labor, the Center for Substance Abuse Treatment, the National Institute on Alcohol Abuse and Alcoholism, and the National Institute on Drug Abuse. We staff both English and Spanish speaking information specialists who are skilled at recommending appropriate publications, posters, and videocassettes, conducting customized searches, providing grant and funding information, and referring people to appropriate organizations. They are available at 1-800-729-6686 to take your calls Monday through Friday from 8 a.m. to 7 p.m. E.S.T., or you can leave an order on voice mail after hours. Or try the online catalog at http://www.health.org. To place an order choose 'publications,' then double click on the NCADI icon, and follow the instructions for ordering publications."

"Learning to Live Drug Free: A curriculum Model for Prevention" from SAMHSA's National Clearinghouse for Alcohol and Drug Information Publications Catalog Fall 1998 from the US Department of health and Human Services, Substance Abuse and Mental Health Services Administration (SAMHSA). Check out page 2, under "Educators" in a 1992 best seller that was designed for grades K-3 (order no. RP0894); grades 4-6 (RPPO 896), and grades 9-12, (RPO897).

"Making the Grade: A Guide to School Drug Prevention Programs," from Drug Strategies, 2445 M Street, NW, Suite 480, Washington, DC 20007 (202 663 6090) Fax 202-663-6110.

Write to the National Clearinghouse for Alcohol And Drug Information, PO Box 2345, Rockville, MD 20847-2345 or call 1-800-729-6686 or 301-468-2600. Be sure to have the complete information on an order, and present yourself as a part of a community . . . not a single user of the information.

For multi-cultural communities try CSAP Cultural Competence Series 1: Cultural Competence for Evaluators: A Guide for Alcohol and Other Drug Abuse Prevention Practitioners Working with Ethnic/Racial Communities (1992, CSAP 206 pp. BD222.

In California check out Alcohol and Drug Prevention (ADP) prevention programs in "Children, Youth, Families and Communities

Division that presents prevention programs for high-risk youth, technical assistance for communities and public education campaigns. Call the Department of Alcohol and Drug Programs 916-/445-0834 or 1-800-879-2772.

For help in violence prevention in California call the Department of Education, School Safety and Violence Prevention Office, 916/657-2989.

For more information about IDEA '97 statute and implementing regulations, contact the Department of Education at (202 205-5465 or (202)-5507 or try www.ed.gov/offices/OSERS/IDEA or www.ideapractices.org—look under Education Department Rules.

14217-PIER

APPENDIX C

Programs to Teach Parenting Skills HIPPY, PAT, BEEP, Head Start, Zero to Three

PAT or Parents As Teachers: Department of Elementary and Secondary Education, PO. Box 480, Jefferson City, Missouri 65102-0480. Phone (314) 751-2095 for PAT information & training programs. See the books by PAT founder, Professor Burton White. Also *Schools That Work*, US Department of Education.

Home/School Partnerships and the Home Instruction Program for Preschool Youngsters: HIPPY Theory and Practice (1993), HIPPY USA, 53 West 23rd Street, 6th floor, New York, NY, 10010.

Ready to Learn: A Mandate for the Nation. A Report of the Carnegie Foundation for the Advancement of Teaching, Princeton, New Jersey: Princeton University Press.

Head Start-type Programs: Organizations: International Child Resource Institute, 1810 Hopkins, Berkeley, CA 94707, (510) 644-1000. National PTA, 330 Wabash St., Suite 2100, Chicago, Ill 60611-3604, (312) 670-6782.

Designs for Change, 6 N. Michigan, No. 1600, Chicago, IL 60602, (312) 857-9292.

National Coalition for Parent Involvement in Education, Box 39, 1201 16th St., NW, Washington, DC 20036, (202) 884-8215.

Family Focus, 310 South Peoria St., Suite 401, Chicago, IL 60607-3534, (312) 421-5200.

Zero to Three—"Tools for working with infants and toddlers with special needs and their families from ZERO TO THREE—the nation's leading resource on the first three years of life." Some of the variety of books offered include: *New Visions for the Developmental Assessment of Infants and Young Children. Coping in Young Children: Early Intervention Practices to Enhance Adaptive Behavior and Resilience. The Emotional Life of the Toddler. Children in Violent Society—and many more.* Zero to Three, 734 15th Street, NW, Suite 1000, Washington, DC 20005-1013

APPENDIX D

PARENT-SCHOOL ORGANIZATIONS

Parents for Public Schools, Inc., (PPS) National Office, 1520 North State Street, Jackson, MS 39202, or call (601) 354-1220, or fax (601) 353-0002, e-mail ppschapter@aol.com.

1. America Goes Back to School Partners' Activity Kit 1996-1997, US Department of Education. Part of the Partnership for Family Involvement in Education; call 1-800-LEARN or http://www.ed.gov/Family/agbts. They recommend:

   > Making our schools safe, disciplined and drug-free
   >
   > Supporting parent and family involvement.
   >
   > Becoming a reading, literate society.
   >
   > Reaching for new levels of excellence with high standards and real accountability.
   >
   > Making technology available so all children will succeed in the 21st century.
   >
   > Preparing young people for careers.
   >
   > Making college more accessible.

2. Ways for Families to Get Involved in Children's Learning. (Examples are given of communities that developed programs to achieve the goals in number 1.)

   CENTER ON FAMILIES, COMMUNITIES, SCHOOLS &

CHILDREN'S LEARNING. John Hopkins University A list of publications covering the following broad areas:

a. Family Education and Training in Early Care and Education.

b. Multicultural Studies of Family Support for Young Children's Success.

c. Partners in Learning: Family Literacy Programs.

d. Studies of Parent Centers in Schools.

e. Parent Information for School Choice. This includes a video CFCVIDI. Building Community: How to Start a Family Center in Your School. VHS 20 minutes, 1992, $15.00.

3. Studies of Policies to Increase Family-School-Community Partnerships

Write to: Publications Department, Attention: Center on Families, Communities, Schools, & Children's Learning, John Hopkins University, 3505 North Charles St., Baltimore, MD 21218-2498.

231

INDEX

absent fathers 103

abusing the fetus 186

ACLU 148

Accountability Report Card 153, 154

Afro-American education 92, 93, 95

aids 139

administration costs 104

"A Nation at Risk: The Imperative for Educational Reform" (National Commission on Excellence in Education) August 26, 1981 39, 40

APA (American Psychological Assoc.) 30

Aristotle 69, 152

At Risk Children 18

basic school 126

Basuk, Ellen 201

BEEP Brookline Early Education Program 176

behavior problems 17

Bell, Terrel, Secretary. of Education. 39

Boros, Oskar K. *Mental Measurement Yearbook* 56

Bowers, C.A. 15, 25

Brookline Early Education Program (BEEP) 176, 177

Brunner, Jerome 194

Bush, George, President 14

business help in school 169

Business Programs 170

Carnegie Commission 41

Caster, Robert L. 90, 91

Chase, Bob NEA president 81

cheating 58

child abuse 111

Charter Schools 145

Clinton, W. J. 20, 43, 131, 164

coercion 28

Common Cause 196

Community Learning Center (CLC) 199, 200, 201, 202

competitive learning 96

corporal punishment 29, 30
counselor 161
curriculum 136

Darwin, Charles 113
democracy 85, 185
domestic violence 112
Down Syndrome 75
dropouts 49, 50, 162, 194
drugs 119, 190
drug babies 116, 117
drug users 190
Dryden, John 172

early education 18, 178
ECFE (Early Childhood Family Education) 178
Edelman, Marian Wright 152
Einstein, Albert 63
elections 86
emotional maturity 138
employment skills 62
employment 141
Epstein, Joyce John Hopkins University 169
ESL (English as a Second Language) 92, 93
Even Start 182
expulsion 33

Family Resources Coalition 140
fathers 100, 103
Fathers (Los Angeles Dads 186
Feldman, Sandra 48

Fetal Alcohol Syndrome (FAS) 100, 101
financing school reform 167
Finn, Chester 42
Forgione, Pascal U. S. Commissioner of Ed. Statistics. 55
Friedenberg, Edgar 15, 116
Frostman, Theodore J. 148
funding, legal actions 106
business 107
federal 108
school 101, 103

Gardner, David Pierpont 39
gifted 36
Glasser, William 71, 85, 159
Goleman, Daniel *Emotional Intelligence* 138
good teachers 133, 134
Gould, Steven Jay *The Mismeasure of Man* 92
grandmothers 179

Head Start 182
herpes, type 2 139, 140
Hidden Curriculum 24
High School Exit Exam. 44
HIPPY (Home Instruction Program for Preschool Youngsters) 174, 175
Hobson v Hansen 94
Holt, John 145
Home Schooling 121
homework 159

Honig, B. Y. 89
HSEE (High School Exit Exam) 44

IDEA (Individuals with Disabilities Education Act) 80, 82
IEP (Individual Education Plan) 77, 78, 79
Illich, Ivan 24
illiteracy 83
inept teachers 16, 131
infant learning 173
internet 144

Jefferson, Thomas 164

learning mythology 25
legal actions 106
LEP (Limited English Proficiency) 16, 45
Locke, John 48, 163

Madison, James 85, 195
Magnet School 127
Maistre, Joseph 90
Maslow, Abraham 199
middle income children 115
Mill, John Stewart 13, 122, 126

NAEP (National Assessment of Education Progress) 52, 104
NASP (National Association of School Psychologists) 29, 33

National Center for Educational Statistics 84
National Institute of Health 83
National Marriage Project, Rutgers Univ. 99
NEC 64, 66

obedience 27
Oakland, Thomas (Nonbiased Assessment) 91

Panetta, Leon 117
Parents as Teachers (PAT) 173
Parents for Public Schools (PPS) 164, 165
Parks, Rosa 90
Patasky, George 185
PBS 50, 152
P.E. 142
Personal Education Program (PEP) 137
Planned Parenthood, Action Fund Inc. 181
PL 94-142 106
Plutarch 63
Political Action Committee 88, 89
Postman, Neil & Charles Weingartner *Teaching as a Subversive Activity* 1968 98
poverty 113, 114, 189
pregnancy problems 99, 100
principal 154
problem children 143

Project STAR (Student-Teacher Achievement Ratio) 133
PSAC Parent-School Advisory Committee 14, 81, 163, 192

quality schools 71
quality teachers 68, 69

raising children 140
reading data 38, 84
Reagan, Ronald President 164
reform 129
Reich, Robert Secretary of Labor 88
Reinquist, William Chief Justice 118
retention 31
Riley, Richard Education Secretary 80, 90, 149
Rogers, Carl 136
Rosenthal *Pygmalion in the Classroom* 160
Rossell, Christine 93
Russell, Bertrand *Education and the Good Life* 209

SAT scores 60, 61
Saturday Review 49
school accountability 153
school funding 101, 105
Schwebel, Milton *Who Can Be Educated?*
Seaborg, Glenn T. 41
sexual maturity 139

Shaw, George Bernard 172
SIDS (Sudden Infant Death Syndrome) 101
Silberman, Charles 25
Sixty Minutes 193
smoking 101
social sense 138
special education 73, 74, 76
Stanford Binet (IQ test) 57
Strong Family—Strong School, U.S. Dept. of Educ. 189

teacher 64, 65, 66, 70, 152 158
teaching techniques 134,
teaching reform 128, 129, 130
teenage pregnancy 99, 100, 183, 184, 185
testing 19, 26, 42, 43
tests 52, 54
achievement 56
aptitude 56
intelligence (IQ) 57
textbooks 35, 54, 85
Third International Math & Science study 55
time in school 130
Title I 168
transition grant 168
TV 112
Twain, Mark 42

U.S. Department of Education 75, 135

violence 109, 111, 112, 187
Vote Smart 197
voting 86, 87
vouchers 147

Walton, John T. Wal-Mart 148
White Flight 120
Whitehead, Alfred N. 11, 72, 128
Wiengartner, Charles 98

Zero Tolerance 34